Horse Heroes
How They Save Us

Mary Hicks

D1736106

BLOOMERY FORGE PRESS

WINTON-SALEM, NC. USA

Copyright © 2021 by **Mary Hicks**

All rights reserved. No part of this publication may be reproduced, distributed, or transmitted in any form or by any means, without prior written permission.

Mary Hicks/Bloomery Forge Press
1814 W. Academy Street
Winston-Salem NC, 27103
www.bloomeryforge.com

Publisher's Note: This is a work of nonfiction. The author has made her best effort to recreate events, locations, and conversations from her memories of them. To protect people's privacy, some names and identifying details have been changed.

Book Layout: 2021 Brenda Hicks Nesbitt; Cover Design Stacey Briggs
Cover Background Photo: © Alec Nesbitt.
Cover Photo used with permission: © Elizabeth Lord Photography.

Horse Heroes, Mary Hicks. -- 1st ed.
ISBN 9798761093416

For Seymour, The Mighty, Sacred Clown,
Healer and My Friend.

"When I bestride him, I soar, I am a hawk: he trots the air; the earth sings when he touches it; the basest horn of his hoof is more musical than the pipe of Hermes."
~ William Shakespeare, Henry V

[Prologue]

It is the late 50's in the US.

United States President Dwight D. Eisenhower signs the National Aeronautics and Space Act into law, creating the National Aeronautics and Space Administration, commonly referred to as NASA. It was established on July 29th as an executive branch federal agency with the mission of researching aerospace and the peaceful scientific applications of aeronautics. NASA, a civilian-oriented agency, replaced the National Advisory Committee for Aeronautics which had been more military-based. Upon its creation, President Eisenhower appointed T. Keith Glennan as the first administrator of NASA. [1i]

While in the greater scheme of things these are still not idle landmarks in my family, for the moment, the truth is I am here. In the yard of an undistinguished house, in the most rudimentary of developments, with the design and color repeated every four houses. The yards are sculpted to accommodate a rather steep hill, with a four-to-five-foot drop between each.

It suits my purpose. With these elements, I will prepare. I will train myself. I will be ready.

For the Grand National.[2]

These are efforts which cannot be taken lightly.

Since my poor beleaguered parents cannot afford either a horse, its housing, training, vet bills or any of the long list of expenses I will discover later in life—there is only one thing left to do.

Become one.

It is 1958. A small figure, a scarf tied to the back of her belt, snorts and paws the ground. And no wonder.

The wall stands nearly chest high, built of random bricks and other painfully solid options. It was the last jump of a course I had set myself.

"We" had done more. Running a mile, as best I could figure it, up and down these hills. Drooping from the heat, the distance, and the unforgiving inclines, I would stagger home for lunch.

And then head out again.

There was a drop jump, launching from our front yard, out over the broken-off holly that had served as our Christmas tree that year. Then the greater challenge. Even though the sapling, broken off in an early snowstorm, was lying on its side, it still filled the difference between the yards and then some. Jumping well up and over to land back in my own yard was a challenge and downright scary— but not the worst.

2

A brick wall is celebrated in songs, poems, and often curses. Unyielding, it is the ne plus ultra of things that are designed not to give. To exact a cost. In this case, tender young skin, and lots of it.

There was fear, without a doubt. The wall came right up to my sternum. It was higher than I had ever jumped before—and way less forgiving.

I can remember glancing up to see my mother watching me through the kitchen window. Even now, I can only wonder what she thought of my venture into another species.

The first refusal was nearly inevitable, and almost as equally unallowable. A smart tap of my hand on my thigh had me circling—and squaring up again. A smart smack—and I was off. *And yes, do note that by now I had managed to conflate Grand National Steeple chasing with Grand National showjumping. Truly, what did I know? Save this...*

I saw the next refusal as disqualification in either discipline.

That last stride. When fear has you so squarely in its grip and you push off anyway. Hard, driving into the ground and inexpertly up into the air. But determined. So determined.

My legs begin to tangle at the highest point of the jump, scrambling to avoid the top brick. It scrapes, a little, on the bare skin on the top of my foot.

But I'm clear. That brick is still up. I've done it.

Prancing around there in the side yard winner's circle, hands pumping then slowly stilled into the quiet comfort of a rider's approval, I circled.

There were no judges, no shouting crowd's cheers. And then, even in my imagination, there's nothing outside of what I can see.

Just a girl, in a side-yard. Notions swarming around her head like leaves, like petals. And love.

Where did she go, this brave gallant girl?

[Chapter 1]

> *Bloom where you're planted.*
> *Stella Payton*

Early Fall 2008

What the hell was I doing in Colorado? The dry fields, the rolling brown hills and sharper rises in the distance. None of these spoke to the heart of my inner landscape, but truth be told I wasn't hearing much of anything else, either.

I had initially come west to escape the ever-present reminders of my mom's passing. The horrors and the sweetness of those last years had all become just too much. Alzheimer's is truly its own special hell. But I thought the wide-open skies of The West might be a place to find a release.

I couldn't help but remember all the visions and dreams I had seen decades ago from the back seat of a family car, headed west. Passing through all the canyons and seeing the elders poised on their horses on the tops of palisades. Seeing a white deer vanish before a car could hit it. Now, all that bright hope had faded. Despite our best intentions in moving Dad west, keeping him close, that effort too had eventually failed. Maybe failure isn't the best word, not if something was doomed from the start.

A relentless numbing had overtaken me. I was six kinds of damaged, but too weary to even have noticed. Grief counselors had warned us that it takes two years just to get over the shock—which meant that I was just starting to get over the shock of my mother's passing when we lost our dad, too. While there are those who insist that PTSD can only be the result of a single shock— a solo incident—others recognize that a series of concussive events drumming through an extended period have their own score of damage. But a musical score this was not.

Now, I looked out over the ridge behind me. Dry, dusty, anything but green. Anything but the world I'd grown up in. As always in the late afternoon, the raptors were up riding the thermals—and on the hunt. There were trails up there too, along the edge of the rise. I had seen the big coyotes—or some kind of a canine—trotting along the path and had no doubt they were hunting too. Prey were everywhere, and I was none too sure I wasn't one of them.

So, there was I was. In another backyard. One with no jumps, but plenty of obstacles. And the girl who had so happily jumped clear—was gone.

[Chapter 2]

*Horses carry the wisdom of healing
in their hearts,
and offer it to any human
who possesses the humility to listen.*
~ Unknown

Even though horses were everywhere I looked in my little Colorado town, it took a job to put my feet back on the path again. Yes, I'd been looking online. I'd even stopped at a nearby dressage barn to enquire about lessons.

But nothing quite clicked.

I, along with my sister, write for a living. Marketing pieces, websites, brochures, advertorials. Stuff. With words. The happiest assignments are those magazine articles and travel articles that just happen to focus on and around developments in extraordinary places. It's even better on those occasions when they occupy a lane we enjoy...

The call to write a brochure and website for the Wellington Training Club was one of those. I still loved horses, even though it had been from a distance for the last decades. With a connection to John and Beezie Madden, this project moved that interest up several levels.

Through the office of close friends, Brenda and I wrangled an invitation to Plum Creek Hollow Farm, which imported and trained talented jumpers from Europe, and Germany in particular. We wanted to see what a more intense training program might look like.

First, they toured us through the barn. A then very young and beautiful Con Capilot was having a bath. He was a gorgeous boy, with possibility written all over him. Once outside, we headed for the big arena. The jumps were already set, and soon the young trainer appeared with a horse. We stood beside the jump standard as they circled—and then thundered off the ground right beside us. By now, remote corners of my brain and heart were beginning to fire again.

Jumping—actually on a horse—was something I yearned for, once upon a time. I could remember trotting a cavaleti with a young grey horse who was way more leg than anything else. We fell. It was perhaps inevitable as he had almost no idea where his hooves were even on regular ground, much less trying to create a measured pace without tripping over poles. And it was a heck of a long way down. Things were so much easier when you bounced. And when your heart was whole and resilient as well. Still, little sparks were forming.

When the jumping demonstration was done, B and I hung around chatting with the barn manager and trainer and I mentioned the young Morgan mare I was looking at, maybe more fantasizing about, online. Somehow that was a catalyzing statement—and I found myself holding a piece of paper with a trainer's number on it.

"Promise me you'll call and go meet this trainer."

Clearly my pursuit of the mare was a bad idea, so I did call...

"I have a semi-retired show jumper you might like. His name is Seymour."

I was so ready to fall for a horse that he could have been anything as long as he had the four-legs of a clip-clopping companion. But he was so much more, an answer to a prayer I didn't even know I had asked yet.

A great horse will change your life.
The truly special ones define it.
~ Unknown

[Chapter 3]

Seymour. The Mighty. Jump Master. Reiki Master. Sacred Clown. Horse Hero

I had managed to mislay the actual directions, though was pretty sure I remembered them. Mostly. Finally, I gave up and called, got myself sorted and was only about twenty minutes late.

But I wasn't nervous yet. I remembered the dressage lesson I'd watched where the trainer never went over a walk with her new student for the first few lessons. Instead, they did breathing and relaxation exercises, all geared to getting grounded in the saddle. That seemed like it would be about my speed. Surely this would be the same...

We were trotting within the first ten minutes.

The muscle memories I had doubted before came through for me. I could remember and did keep my hands low and quiet, so they were separate, isolated from the movement of my body. Sort of. My heels were pressed down and fairly steady. All, more or less. And, at the mercy of less than fit muscles. Memories they might have. Endurance, not so much.

On the less positive side, my pants were squeaking. I had stopped off at the riders' consignment shop in Castle Rock the weekend before. For whatever reason, everyone there thought full-seat sticky pants were the way to go. They gave you just that "little extra insurance" against coming out of the saddle. They also gave me a horror of appearing in public in the damned things, at least outside of a barn. I remember when I finally ventured into the local health food store on the way home. Between a balky cart and my still wretchedly squeaking pants, folks were leaning around the corner to see what on earth was approaching. I could find the humor in my various trials, but...

Still. I was nervous. For no clear reason—but those are the kinds of things that twine deep inside you, linking dread and trauma and loss. And fear. As I would learn again and again, Seymour—the Mighty See—was a saint, a comedian, and my heart horse way before I even knew it. But for right now we were getting to know each other. I was getting to know what it was like to be back in the saddle again.

And See had a way of turning his energy up and down so you would only see a part of him at first. I don't really mean his get up and go, but his energy as in his persona. His energy field, as I would come to know it. I thought he was a nice horse. I had absolutely no idea.

"He's trying to make you laugh."

At this point, the trainer was still helping me with tacking and untacking.

I looked up at Seymour goofing around refusing to release the bit.

Yes, he had the bit in his teeth. His eyes were lit up with the fun of it.

And just like that, I fell for a sacred clown.

I wish I could say that I knew at once that I needed him. But the truth was it took a lesson or two. Probably more. But soon enough I would drift off to sleep dreaming of a half-lease, so Seymour could be at least a little bit mine. When I finally got up my nerve to ask about it, couched in a "they wouldn't really want to, would they?" kind of way, it turned out they really would. This was 2008-2009, well into the recession and they had two horses at the barn. Getting a break from even some of the expense was welcome. And I? I was in heaven, even if it was a shaky one.

[Chapter 4]

Early days when the sun was mostly shining

Now as an almost bona fide, almost horse person, I joined my young barn mates on the occasional weekend show outings. These were smaller shows all along the Front Range even in the spring—which is to say those weekends when it wasn't snowing or when the show was indoors. We were an interesting group, composed of young riders, their parents and me with a few adult riders thrown in for good measure. As the season went on my sister began to join us. We would meet up at the barn or at the trailer at the show grounds bearing gifts. Bagels and cream cheese. Homemade gluten-free muffins (my offerings), snacks and juice, of course—but quite often champagne to go along with it. We were a lively group. Flo—then Flora—Shmorgoner showed Seymour and it was always entertaining to hear the announcer's game efforts to get through her name, especially as the pair began winning more and more. Her mother Stella was an enthusiastic supporter and often responsible for the champagne or Kahlua if there was coffee. Samantha Cook, Sammie, rode her own horse Apollo, and they were responsible for a number of ribbons and more substantial winnings as well. I was the cheerleader and happy with that, saluting all our riders but of course my almost horse with all my heart. I'm not sure my neighbors on the bleachers or the rails were always equally thrilled. It's possible they thought I might stop to draw breath somewhere along the line so they might get the chance to extol their own horse or child, but they reckoned without my theatre training.

None the less, I remember these outings as being low-key. Competitive but not daunting. Perhaps this is rose-colored glasses, or Seymour-colored anyway. Every day, with every show I fell more and more in love. Now I could see just how beautiful he was, how elegant in the air—and how much he loved a good jump-off.

The truth was, they did my fractured heart good.

But the lessons in between slowly became more strained. The trainer, a woman who seemed all strength and courage, was running out of patience with my too timid heart. Our early attempts at the canter ended up with me wrapped around See's neck—though I have to say it was a pretty good save even without the now-abandoned sticky pants. The more she pushed the more I froze. I'm sure she would say, and it may well be fair, that if she hadn't pushed, I wouldn't have gotten anywhere. Still, it wasn't my best learning modality—especially when I was still trying to put myself back together after all the trauma. I felt like a ship doing running repairs while bailing.

But there is another, even more powerful truth. I was sticking it out for See. To be with him. Quietly, out towards the pasture when I'd walk him home. In the late afternoons when only a few riders, if any, were in the barn and we had it to ourselves. In the timeless time when a hug, arms around his neck—his neck around mine—was comfort personified. Although I trained in Level 1 reiki some years before, it never occurred to me that we were chakra to chakra. It just was. But things were about to change.

And for better or worse, it mattered.

[Chapter 5]

On Being Immortal

For so many people, the concept of immortality has a heavy involvement with their mother church. Or philosophy. Or wanting to create something so massive, so important that it might never be forgotten. Those weighty efforts and ideas would be shocked to know a truth. When it comes to immortality, nothing gets you closer than being twelve years old—and being on a horse, preferably your own.

We were all immortal, once.

When we fell off, we bounced. When our horse ran away with us, we secretly egged them on, eager for that wild wind on our face and in the tangle of our hair. Jumping whatever stood in our path, our beloved co-conspirators seemed to revel in our adventures, adding their own thunder and grace. Then, these uncaged hearts beat as one.

Because here's another truth. Immortals are wild. Feral. Untamed. It lies at the heart of their being even when seemingly quieted. Years later—perhaps no longer acknowledged—it still lies at the heart of us, waiting. I think this is what The West has always meant to me.

Years later I would meet new Immortals. My stablemates. Young riders who became friends, even though I now knew fear, and was, more often than not, in its thrall. But when they gave me a compliment on my riding, it stuck with me like no other. Still wild to still a little wild, they spoke to me—and I heard them. I am still grateful.

[Chapter 6]

Grabbing Mane and Catching Air

After some months, I was still having a hard time getting ready to go lesson. As much as I was head over heels for my boy, I began to wonder if this was any way to live. So full of fear. I was now quite simply terrified to ride.

Stomach churning, I pulled on my breeches and boots. Zipped up and snapped my half chaps. Clomped down the stairs, my body going forward while my mind was scrambling backwards as fast as it could go. By the time I was on the small winding road that led to Eagle Woman Ranch in Parker, I had made up my mind. This was no way to live. There had to be a change. This was it. I was going to get in or get out, and today's lesson would be the decider.

I had tried. Even with all this, pulling up to the barn was always the best part of the day. Seymour was in the closest paddock. By now, he knew the sound of my engine and always had his head over the fence as I came around the corner. A nicker has to be the nicest sound in the world. It is at once a warm acknowledgement that you are loved and welcome. And known, no longer a stranger. The assumption that you have carrots or something nice goes without saying...and truly is only a little important. To be seen and welcomed by a horse is without equal.

Or at least that is what I would be learning, down the line. For today, my riding fate sat in all our hands, particularly mine—the ones with the sweaty palms. Like every other day, I tacked up, warmed up and prayed that we wouldn't canter.

And yes, that thud was the sound of riders' jaws dropping. For most, cantering is the good part, the reward for surviving untold circles of posting without respite. And posting? That graceful rise out of the saddle and back again, timed to coincide with the outside fore and inside hind, is guaranteed to trash your quads.

But for the first time, the trainer pointed to a jump. Small. Probably an x-rail, though I'm not sure I truly remember.

"Off you go. Just trot him up and grab mane."

As a dancer, at least in my very early days, there was nothing I liked better than to catch a little air. I loved the sweep and stretch of the front leg launching—and the extra stretch in the back. I loved the full stretch and roll through of the foot—and the power of its thunder to launch you off the ground. I just loved the heck out of defying gravity, even for a moment. I even had dreams where I could suspend myself in the air for as long as I liked. There was an extra special stretch, right at the top of the jump that released you from gravity. In my dreams

I could tour around up there for hours, only coming down for the pure joy of jumping up again. So even though I hadn't jumped a horse for years—decades really—and never anything beyond a fallen tree, we were headed up to familiar territory. My place. The air. The one I had made my own in a nondescript backyard with my heart racing. In this arena, on this stage, I had certainly practiced the 2-point again and again. I knew you had to hold yourself there as the horse launched. But this. Not just a static position but soaring alongside a master.

I locked my eyes on the jump as we came around the corner, then lifted my eye line as we got close. Got up out of the saddle and punched my heels down. See never shirked a jump (unless there was water, and that is a different story.) So even with a novice on his back sending him towards a small jump, he would never step over, but always launch up into his perfect arc. Clearly signaling that it was about damned time, he was ready.

I had visualized this so many times, I felt like I had already done it. As we rose, I realized I never had. We jumped a few more times that day, the last set with the immortals—the fearless and accomplished young riders who were the future of this program—called in to watch. How much I loved seeing their eyes open and hearing their sweet congrats and encouragement.

The next lesson we jumped an "in and out" and cantered on to turn back and get the next. Three jumps in a row! Cantering without even thinking. There was so much joy in those first sweet days. Training with him in the arena. Heading out to the shows to cheer on the Immortals, with Flora sometimes riding See. We brought muffins and bagels. Prepping for that day when I too would be in the irons—competing against the 5-year-olds. Ah, well.

And it was weeks, even a few blessed months, before the stomach terrors came back...

[Chapter 7]

Seymour Becomes Mine

The times were still precarious financially. As a once long-time staffer, I had yet to adjust to being a freelancer, and never really knowing when the next job would roll in though we were lucky, for the most part. But the notion of having someone's well-being wholly dependent on me in these conditions wasn't sitting well. By now I had taken on a full lease for See, though not entirely of my own volition. We kept looking for someone to take on the other half—but nothing really clicked. The stress amped up, and then increased again. Another possibility faltered. Another "maybe" failed.

Then the key question was put forward. Would it make a difference if he was my horse? Really mine, wholly and completely? I'm damned if I know why—but of course it did. The income from a cell tower rental could be completely devoted to his care. It wasn't a gigantic amount, but nicely nurtured against reasonable expenses...it would do. My heart began to race again. This beauty, this incomparable creature—to my mind— could be mine.

Of course, it wasn't without difficulty. Definitely not without heartache going the other way. Rachel, See's first rider in the states, daughter of See's owner, hadn't ever imagined that they might let him go. It was part of the barn lore. If nothing else, See would always belong to the Konigsbergs. It wasn't an easy release for her or for any of them, and I am deeply grateful that they saw their way clear. And I have to salute Glee White for leading these negotiations. While we might not have found peace before or after, in this one instance there there was incontrovertible grace—and I am grateful.

We had weeknight gatherings once a month or so, and one happened to coincide with this event. Several of us were doing a jumping lesson and as I took my turns, I could hear the murmurs growing.

"They gave him to her." I patted his neck and got ready to circle again.

"Yes, Seymour!"

"I thought they said they'd never give him up!"

Whoever thinks horses don't hear or aren't even listening is just flat wrong. With every statement, See was just prancing a little more—and walking a little taller. Never one to hide his light under a bushel, I think the boy was happy. I know he was loved.

[Chapter 8]

A Moment

In all these times with my boy, there were always moments. Not life-changing or ribbon-earning or even noticed by anyone but me. The funny part is they were still significant. In the end, I think it is the day to day with a horse that truly mattered.

It's always tactile, this connection. And present. The sound of hooves. Walking beside you, easily. Or picking up the pace. Restless. Ready for the next. Ready to move on. To brace for the next challenge. Fearsome, fearful. Or...

Just walking. Breathing in the steady beat. The scent wraps around you as you embrace this truth. Or simply walk beside it, within it.

You are loved. Nothing fancy. Nothing to lose it over. Just a simple truth.

You are loved.

And in this one moment, it seems irrevocable .

May the day come when you realize it never was.

[Chapter 9]

Jumping At Plum Creek

It was coming again, that time we call spring in Colorado. Others call it late May or even June. But in our world, the important thing was it was show season again, with much to celebrate.

This year some of the larger local barns were hosting invitational shows, with a limited entry. Riders donned their white breeches, and then put sweatpants over them. More formal ribbons were arrayed on tables, class entry prices went up—and nerves did too.

On this lovely morning, I was tooling along some of the back roads of Larkspur, CO, grateful that the traffic nightmare known locally as RenFest had yet to begin. Yet as I got closer to the pickup point for my dear friend Elizabeth Scott, it did seem we were slowing down courtesy of all the cyclists. Now with weather like this and roads like these, it wasn't unusual to see folks out with their bikes. Elizabeth hopped in and we were off again—for a minute. But wait? Was there actually someone directing traffic at the idyllic junction of Perry Park Ave and State Highway 105? And were they saying that the cars should stop, and all the nice cyclists should keep going?

Well, of course they were. We were now caught up in the long loop of the Elephant Rock Cycling Race. When I first moved to Castle Rock, friends told me to prepare for this event much like one would a blizzard. Stock up on food. Hit the liquor store and the library—though not necessarily in that order. Check and see what was on tv, and, if necessary, order a new service. And then, whatever you do, do not leave your house! Obviously, I had gotten caught up in the anticipation of seeing Flo and the Mighty compete again and showing him off to my fellow horse enthusiast—and I would pay a price.

105 is the winding home of a number of beautiful farms and ranches, including Plum Creek Hollow Farm which was hosting this weekend's show. While the cyclists were supposedly racing, they weren't exactly hustling. Nor were they wholly gracious. Every now and again one group would grudgingly wave you around and there would be 70 exhilarating yards—before you had to creep again. Elizabeth was coaching me in deep breathing and other relaxation techniques by the time we came in sight of the farm. The nice thing about Plum Creek is that you do get a glimpse of it well before the entry gates, and sure enough there were the horse trailers parked on the edge of the farm road with horses' heads peeking out of every window. They clearly were fascinated by what the humans were getting up to now.

Our barn had brought the horses over the day before so the riders could have a practice day, and everyone could have a chance to settle in. Elizabeth and I hiked in and looked around through the temporary stalls. Then one horse turned and looked at me. Of course.

My sister and I had gone to a show at the Horse Park in the early days. I knew our trailer would be parked near the back gate of the park but hadn't been able to find it so we started out on the dirt road towards the rings. There was a field with a bit of a gully between the road and the trailers. I could see a beautiful bay tied to the side of the last trailer over there. And then he turned and looked at me. Of course. From across a field or in a welter of stalls...

But now it was time to get ready. For the riders to lose the sweats. For us to help the Immortals brush off their jackets and do a final polish on the other gleaming hides. To check that hairnets were nicely tucked up and manes were as smooth as they would get. One by one they headed for the mounting block and then they were away.

There was a little grandstand and Elizabeth and I scrambled up. We had a perfect view of the course and of the waiting areas. A "friend of the barn" rider was there with his big horse, who made See and most of the other horses look like ponies. But despite the size difference, and some more experienced duos out there, our teams looked ready to go. There was no more turning to look.

We were sprinkled among some 20-25 entries. For this day there was no arena. Instead, they were competing over jumps on grass on a kind of Derby field. It was groomed to perfection, verdant and gorgeous—not words that usually came to mind in Colorado. Still, there were the usual breakdowns and near catastrophes. Young riders didn't quite live up to their show dreams and retired near tears. A few moved through the course like a wrecking ball. Another rider came off over a jump. She managed to keep hold of the reins but unfortunately the bridle came off with her. Where upon her horse chose to explore this new field in a merry canter. The grooms and grounds people seemed less enchanted but finally captured him. The entries kept coming, many with good trips as well.

Finally, there they were. I'm sure there were days when Flo was as nervous as the next rider—she just didn't show it. And See? He came prancing out, eyes sparkling with the light of battle, a happy warrior in his chosen arena. They circled, picked up a canter and they were off, smooth as silk rippling and flowing over the jumps. They were quick too and held the winning time almost to the end. For all his competitive ferocity, Seymour was a graceful jumper who seemed to count his own strides—I never saw him put a foot wrong, anyway.

The final competitor was not a natural jumper, to put it politely. Fancy he was not. He was the only horse I ever saw jump with his legs straight out in front of him.

There were so many near wrecks that I was watching with my eyes half covered and Elizabeth was gasping at every approach. But here's the thing. The rider had a hell for leather approach to this whole "English" thing and her quarter horse was just the guy to take it home. Pretty they were not—but they were .25 seconds faster than Flo and See. We didn't grudge them their win—hell, we were glad they made it around the course in one piece. But not everyone was so forgiving...

[Chapter 10]

A Word from The Man

It occurs to me that this story is not complete. That a certain lightness of touch—or outright slapstick is missing.

Because this...

For all that See was a Reiki Master, and a Jump Master and God only knows whatever other masteries he rolled with, not to mention being the King of Hearts, he was one thing more.

A Sacred Clown. From the horse's mouth....

Fun Things to do with your human.
A Primer for Sacred Clowns
and Other Fun-Loving Horses.
By Seymour Konigsberg Hicks.

I like to make people laugh. I like a good laugh myself, like getting in a fine roll in the mud down at the bottom of the hill even as my rider sprinted across the pasture to come get me. And was there any expression of affection better than snuggling my beautiful muddy head into their clean shirt—after making sure to rub it up and down those new breaches too?

Of course, there's always this trick. After your friend has brushed out all the mud, or the shedding coat—or both—and swept the floor to leave the crosstie ready for the next rider; after you are tacked up and start to walk to the arena— hopefully almost an equal distance from the shovel in the arena and the one in the wash stall—you may then relieve yourself. Ho, the whole barn will be laughing with you.

Once in the arena, when you're bored of standing out of the way watching all the other horses go, why not grab a jacket off a handy post and flap it all around? This has the advantage of bringing all the attention back to you, where it belongs, while also creating some great stretches for your rider as the she tries desperately to get it away from you.

Big fun!

Then, once it's your turn, be sure to pay very close attention to your rider's every cue. In the flurry that they create, there's bound to be one that could signal something you'd like to do. For example, my rider Mary tended towards a shallower turn going into the jump. One day, she really cut it close—and you know what that means!!

JUMP-OFF, BABY! TURN AND BURN! Blast off the ground, get part of your turn in the air and GO! I like to think she secretly enjoyed it, once she stopped that wheezing sound from hitting her sternum on my neck. I mean, she did say she wondered what it would be like to ride a show course with me....

And shows are a great place to add a little fun to your winning ways. First, as soon as you get on the grounds, let 'em know you're here. It serves notice to your rivals, lets your friends know you're onsite, and most importantly takes your rider's mind off their nerves as they try to figure out how to get you to pipe down.

But always be gracious, even if the judge mistakenly pins the wrong horse. If you're like me, you can correct this travesty by accelerating and passing the horse wearing the blue ribbon in the victory gallop around the Derby Field. Show them a clean pair of heels and lead the way!

These are just a few tips on how to bring joy or at least a laugh to the one that loves you. You know what they say...laughter is the best medicine. So Sacred Jump Master Clown Reiki Healer is now my preferred title! Thoughts?

[Chapter 11]

Joy Is So Fleeting. And Ambition Yearns Onward

We had made our way through a few barns now. It was probably inevitable that we would end up at the Colorado Horse Park. It was, or at least seemed the ne plus ultra of the Front Range, and our trainer's ambition. She had been working to collect the kind of clientele that combined talent, and determination with the wherewithal to support an ambitious program. Horses sourced to compete from the best in the states, and eventually abroad. Riders who could afford to support the whole HITS season with their horses based in California while they jetted back and forth.

Unfortunately, not all of us could keep up.

In March of 2012 I gave away my best friend—even though I didn't know that yet... You see, I didn't know my horse loved me too. After three years as a neophyte in the show horse world I had run out of money, hope and endurance. But even this desperate save wasn't easy.

A rehab barn in Santa Fe had agreed to take him in. They would pick him up Thursday March 1st. On February 29th—a leap year of course—I went to say goodbye.

It was as hard as it gets. Horses read people as easily as I read a favored author. They know when you're stressed but they don't know why, which can make it even more terrifying for them. So, it was critical to get all my emotions in check—to hold hard. I didn't want to scare him. Alarm him. Make this leave taking as hard for him as it was for me. I just wanted sunshine to pour through my eyes and hands as I said goodbye--only I wasn't letting that word out of the bag either. I thought...

But March 1st came and went as the rehab barn delayed a week. On March 7th, I said goodbye again. For no apparent reason because they couldn't come this time either. On March 15th I hauled myself to the barn for one last farewell. This was it. Seymour wouldn't even look at me this time. My attempts to hold the line were looking ragged too. But he finally accepted a treat. And of course, they were delayed one more day. But I had said my last goodbye.

[Chapter 12]

The Return of The Mighty

I had meant to be brave.

In private, I had howled and eventually become silent again. I raged that I was not rich and couldn't afford to keep him—but once again realized I would trade my life for no other. I ached and there was no answer, save more pain. I missed See so but could only hope it was going well for him.

When the news first broke that he would become a therapy horse See's show rider, Flo Schmorgoner's first reaction was telling. "Seymour? A therapy horse?? Isn't he a little... competitive?"

It was true that See would still race his competition even in the after-class victory gallop. And that his triumphant bellows are probably still painfully ringing in the ears of any attending the same show. But I pinned my hopes on his other sustaining characteristic—his great heart. Surely, he would reach out to those in need as he always had. Certainly, he would not let wounded beings falter.

I wasn't at the barn anymore, so I didn't hear a lot of scuttlebutt. Occasionally I would hear that See was doing ok. That one of the trainers there, also a German, had him out on trail rides. As a show horse, this was not necessarily his strong suit but a good way to keep him fit and relaxed.

Then gradually the news began to change. Maybe this wasn't working out as well as hoped. Maybe he was a little big for the side-walkers. Or a little quick. I don't really know what happened. They said in the end that they couldn't really use him. By then, I didn't really care.

After eight weeks, See was coming home. My bank account had recovered enough that I could take care of him, at least if he was out to pasture. A new healing path lay before him, though neither of us knew about that yet either. I only knew this. Even though he was due in on a Friday evening, it was Saturday before I got confirmation he was there, at the barn. At the Colorado Horse Park, a main entrance to the barns took you through to the door to the first passageway between the two indoor arenas. You yelled "Door", and if no one yelled back you proceeded.

Only this time it was horse yelling back at me.

"Seymour?"

The shriek became a nicker. An unmistakable nicker. A voice that I knew pretty much like I knew my own. The thing was, he knew my voice too. I shoved on through the next door and there he was. Mashing himself up against the sides of the stall. Getting as close as he could. My boy. My beloved. I mashed myself up against the sides of the stall too. Soon, our ruckus brought others. The Coors, who had had their first lessons on him. More riders from our aisle in the barn, mashing in too. This horse was loved.

But it was only then that I realized how much he loved back. Over the next couple of days, when I took him out to hand graze to prep him for pasture living after arid New Mexico, he would be a little on the muscle. But he would always tap in to make sure I knew he meant no harm. Touch his muzzle to my shoulder or even my hand. And then he would be dancing again. Even though the increments gradually increased, the end of each session would find him grazing between my feet. And the boisterous answers to my shout of "Door?" were ever more joyful, ever more concrete. It was a fine truth and very clear. My boy loved me just as I loved him.

It was now that a new path began to open—even though it just looked like an old pasture in a near abandoned venture. We never really know, do we...?

[Chapter 13]

An Introduction to Reiki

I first met Bev Petty in NYC in the early 90's. A friend of friends from the NC School of the Arts, she was now practicing massage and—as it turned out—Reiki. It was my first introduction to this amazing practice and a welcome one.

Some years earlier in Norway, probably a decade or two, I had managed to flip myself upside down and land on my neck on the basement bannister after a day out skiing. Somehow, I did not break anything, but the muscles would spasm at the slightest provocation for years. I'm pretty sure this particular episode started when a bag lady walloped me in the back of the head. I had mentioned that she might not want to be out in traffic on 57th Street. She bared her teeth and snarled at me. Pretty sure she hissed, too. Suit yourself, I said and walked on. Lesson: never turn your back on folks who respond like a big, feral cat. Now I was hurting, once again, and looking for help.

Bev's studio may have been in Hell's Kitchen, but it was wonderfully welcoming for anyone weary of pain. After settling myself in on the table, Bev asked if I'd like her to add Reiki in as well, explaining it was a kind of healing energy work. At that point, I would have tried anything, but this Reiki thing sounded good.

How lightly we sometimes enter our most important path.

As I drifted away, and the pain dissipated, I slid straight into a vision. I was in a kind of tunnel underground and starting to climb out. The ladder was roughly cobbled together, and the upward passage wasn't much better. Roots hadn't quite been cleared and it seemed like the ladder went on forever. In fact, it was going on forever. There seemed to be no last step. Then I realized the last step was simply to become, to be. With that thought I was out and in the middle of a wide, gently rolling green plain. I could hear a faint jingling sound off in the distance and, yes, hooves. As they got closer, ever so slowly, I could see these beautiful horses were wearing decorated harnesses of some sort. Tiny bright bells were stitched into the edge of saddlecloths and reins. Beautiful, vivid colors became clear as they approached. And one more thing was obvious. One horse had no rider. The one they were leading to me. A beautiful silvery grey, he was the horse of my dreams. I mounted and we were off, with a gait that flowed over every rise and fall of this land. After a long, long run I could finally see something beyond this endless green horizon. A shimmering blue lake. Truthfully, I was disappointed that this journey would end—or at least change once we got to the water. But his stride did not slacken as he strode onto the water and ran lightly across the top. We were still galloping on water as the vision gently vanished.

This was not the last vision I had during Reiki, but it certainly was a key one. Something I was only to begin to understand later.

Bev told me her Reiki Master was coming to town, from Cleveland of all places, and really encouraged me to go take lessons. Not that I have anything really against Cleveland, but it never really struck me as a place that could nurture these kinds of off-beat miracles.

Have I mentioned how very wrong I can be?

Long story somewhat short, I signed up for the workshop. It would be held over a weekend in Manhattan. As a parent in Connecticut with shared custody, weekends were always precious time—or just ordinary days that one dragged oneself through—depending on if my son was with me or not. This was one of the latter, so I was happy to at least be doing something.

Meeting a Reiki Master

I wasn't expecting a tailored woman in a business suit, which only goes to show how prejudiced we each might truly be. There were probably 12-14 of us in the room—a spacious West Side apartment with all its furniture shoved to the walls. Most of my fellow students were women—and nurses.

I don't remember how many exercises we did, guided meditations really—but I do remember one. We were to be walking down a road or a path of our choosing, one that we might especially like. And as we walked stress would fade away, leaving us both stronger and more relaxed. Closing our dream eyes, we were to notice everything—the sounds, the scents, the air itself, the temperature, even the quality of the light around us. When we "opened" those eyes, there before us would be our enemy, or one who had done us harm... We were to reach out to them, make peace with them, but not let them go until they gave us a gift. I particularly loved the notion of the gift. Not simply because I'm always happy with a nice pressie—but because it seemed like it sealed the deal so to speak, that all enmity would always be held at bay by that simple act. That the relationship itself would be shifted, which was an interesting lesson.

But the key part of these two days were the four attunements.

While there are Reiki courses that plow through levels one and two in a single weekend, and I'm sure that works well for some, it wasn't a path for me. The attunements are meant to align your energy with Reiki. The word Reiki simply means universal energy. But there are other translations that I'm particularly fond of: "Rei means "*the wisdom of God*" and Ki means "*life force*" or "*energy.*" Combined the meaning of Reiki can be translated as "*spiritually guided life force*" .[3]

It's important to remember that Reiki is largely an oral tradition, passed only from master to student for a long time. Much like, but not a bit like a game of gossip, things shift in the telling. As such, it's not surprising that variations have popped up, sometimes each with their passionate advocates. But when there are those who insist that their path is the only path, and that "their reiki" is the only Reiki, I begin to part company with them. In my now longer practice, I've come to believe that Reiki is just love, practiced in alignment with the highest energy. Early in my life I was lucky enough to encounter the concept of agape—thank you Reverend William Merrill from the North Carolina School of the Arts. His class was a virtuoso telling of comparative religion and it has been printed on all my days—but I digress. Agape is Greek, one of the four forms of love—eros, filios, storge and agape. (Yes, there are more, but these were his focus.) In his telling, agape is love without boundaries. Without need for an equal response, and definitely without demand.

"This is the love that one might have for every member of humanity. It involves compassion and empathy and is a very encompassing concept. In Christianity, the word agape is used to describe the unconditional love of God toward believers, as well as the love believers have for God."[4]

Being young in the sixties and a hippie awash in a revolution of love, I tried to practice agape in the world in the world of men and women. I largely crashed and burned—and rightly so. I don't think we're meant to love a partner wholly unselfishly. After all, it is as a "self" that we love and are loved.

But in Reiki, and all energy work, I found a home for this love. Some twenty-odd years later, I was volunteering in a yoga studio in Colorado, trading classes for taking care of the front desk. There were practitioner/therapists upstairs and we got one session each month from either a masseuse, or a hypnotherapist—or the resident Reiki Master, Erin Keefe-Feiner.

It was no wonder that my hands started to light up again. They wanted to go back to work. I decided to start from scratch with Erin, repeating Reiki Level 1 and going on from there. In general, there are 3 levels of Reiki, depending on which branch of Reiki you study. Mine is Usui and in that Level 1 is the basics of learning the protocol and the energy. In Level 2 you learn the symbols that focus and strengthen your practice and allow you to work as a professional. Level 3 is becoming a Reiki Master. That would be my eventual path, some years later.

The truth is, Reiki simply makes me happy, sometimes even exuberantly so. Early on, I used to worry if the energy would come, would it be there for me and my clients, horse or human. But I can also remember my first "client". In my tradition of Usui Reiki, case studies are critical. For Level 1, you needed five. My master recommended this woman to me. A breast cancer survivor, the woman was now post-surgery for brain cancer and facing radiation therapy.

And I was absolutely terrified.

"Throw me off the cliff much?"

Erin laughed and then told me that I could do no harm. And she told me that when this woman approached her needing help but with her resources exhausted, my face floated up before her-Erin. Very well. If I might be of service...

I prepped the room carefully, clearing and cleansing every nook and cranny physically and spiritually. When my client arrived, I got her settled on the table, made sure my notes were close at hand—and had my first classic panic attack.

"Please let me be..." *Oh lordie, where is the energy? The answer came. Chant her name.* " a true vessel" *Oy oy oy, Where is it? Answer? Hush!* "of the sacred reiki energy!" Still chanting to myself, I began to settle and let my hands listen and speak. When I practice now, I've realized at its essence I'm simply pouring love on my clients and truly there is an endless supply. Because in the end, it's not about me. So, my prayer is always "Please let me be a true vessel of the sacred Reiki energy." A vessel, anointed by a horse.

But that story comes a little bit later...

For now, it was horses themselves that I was concerned for. Seymour with his tricky ankle. His pasture mates and their various ailments. All were either retired or on pasture rest. Now, I wanted to learn about all the ways to heal them. The ways they would heal me would be revealed in its own time.

[Chapter 14]

Winsome Farms. A New Home and Another New Start.

If you drive out Ridge Road in Castle Rock, past a smattering of stores and around the roundabout, the view on your right opens dramatically. You look out over a valley to the Rampart Range and the Fourteeners beyond. You'll also, if you go just far enough, see Winsome Farms.

When the trainer decided the somewhat rundown farm where the retirees and Seymour boarded should become a polo training center and that all of us had to clear out—Winsome took us in on short notice.

I had already been lessoning there—so of course they had already heard an earful of Seymour's charms, but he did settle in on his best behavior. Soon, they began to put more experienced riders on him to see how he would do—and he did well.

Finally, I got my chance. It was as if we'd never stopped. He still would reach around and touch my boot when we paused. He still loved pole work—and so did I. But when push came to shove, I was still scared. I just couldn't pull the trigger and canter.

Even now, even after all this, I want nothing more than to apologize to him. For believing more in fear than I believed in him. At least in the saddle. On the ground, things were starting to change.

[Chapter 15]

Equine Reiki. A New Mastery Pursued

Erin Keefe-Feinner. I have seen her as a kindly practitioner and Reiki stalwart. She has been my rock when I was in a hard place. She supported me in difficult times with my beloved animals. I have also seen her as a wild Irish priestess summoning up her power as I worked across from her on a client.

She is my Reiki master. And now we had a new journey together.

As before, my hands had been calling out, this time to work on the horses—but I didn't know who I could find to teach me in the timeframe I wanted. I had looked at Anna Twinney, the best-known Equine Reiki Master and practitioner in our part of Colorado, but her next course was full. The one after that was just too far away not to mention too far in the future.

Patience has never been a strong suit.

Nor, apparently, was seeing what was right in front of me. Of course, Erin could and would teach me Equine Reiki. She had done her Reiki Master project on it. We found a day that would work for both of us. Unfortunately, we didn't think to check the weather.

It was late fall, near winter, pretty much the same thing in Colorado. In a word, cold. Winsome Farms is perched on a ridge just above Castle Rock, with an unimpeded view of the Rampart Range and the Rockies beyond. Also unimpeded? The wind. So, all in all just a perfect day to learn equine reiki outdoors, as long as you have a great barn jacket, super warm sweater, thick scarf, serious gloves and or mittens, a superb hat, and a crazed determination to master this.

We began with my own Seymour and his pasture mates but before we started, we asked permission. From the horses. Exactly as one would with humans, asking permission of an "animal" is a courtesy honoring the sovereign nature of these beings. You can ask permission through various forms of muscle testing. In its simplest form, you stand up straight in an easy balance facing the horse, close your eyes and ask. If you find yourself leaning or even stepping forward, it's a yes. Otherwise, it's a no, or more gently not now or not yet. I know it might seem ridiculously easy to manipulate the answer, but it isn't. Horses will let you know, one way or another.

Rallying around the hayrack, this group could seem to care less about our efforts. Enthralled with their feed, though, they were the perfect first subjects. Calm, willing and mostly standing still. After I learned the process and equine chakra points, Erin left me to practice on See while she dealt with the other horses who began trying to muscle in. And who could blame them? My first learning was that as herd animals, horses share energy. When I worked on See, I could see his pasture mates start to relax and release.

As a deep contentment spread throughout this mini-herd, I first learned to breathe in the profound peace of Equine Reiki. It is, but it isn't, but it IS a whole different experience from working with people. Horses, even those who have no real reason to trust people, accept the energy fairly quickly. Their breath slows and deepens—and so does yours. When they sigh, you know you're in. There are some who test your boundaries too, but gently. I still learn something new every time, but this first time was magic.

Still, I was grateful when we moved to the horses that were stalled inside. Winsome Farms is an older barn and training center built on a far more ancient Native American campground. While not the fanciest show barn on the Front Range, it has a deep resonance from both those much older times and the barn's own decades old, single-family owned history. And on one side of the barn, it also had heat.

I already had permission from Shannon Gossman and Matt Davis to work with their wonderful horses Rocco and Kato—and now I almost had the feeling back in my fingers. The idea was that I would practice a full session with supervision on the first of them and tackle the second on my own while Erin was still in hailing distance.

While both of these horses changed over the time that I knew them, on this day Rocco was sweet as pie and almost as brave. Like most warmbloods, he's a good-sized horse but I'm not sure he believes that. In his heart, he was a cautious, perhaps even timid spirit. But in this, he had a gift for me. It was called "slow down." He clearly was not a fan of "new" things. But once I took the time to breathe with him and even more time to move slowly from chakra to chakra, he sighed and settled into the process. Which brought up a new "learning" opportunity.

The young horse in the next stall, the one at the head of a line of stalls, had had enough. Was he not in the Stall of Honor, the first that any would see upon entering the barn? Perhaps not everyone saw the stall order in this light—but no matter. Whatever this new thing was, this new form of human attention, he wanted some. He deserved it. Now. Racket ensued. Erin dispatched herself to go work with him through the bars at the front of the stall. That worked well enough until she started to step away as I moved on to Kato.

Blammo. Blammo. Double blammo. Hooves on stall walls can make quite the statement. His was quite simple. HUMAN WILL REMAIN WITH ME!

I moved on to Kato on my own, as of course it was meant to be all along. A five-year old Danish Warmblood, he had only been imported a few months before but already showed signs of what he would become.

Gifted and preternaturally poised for so young a horse, he welcomed this new opportunity. He seemed to take pride in this dance, leaning a shoulder in for more energy or moving a hip away when he was done.

Later, this early interaction would serve us both well. I remember waking up early one Saturday morning some months later. A whole two days free of deadlines stretched before me. Normally this would be a fine reason to turn over and go back to sleep. Or get up, let the dogs out, feed everybody—and then go back to sleep. But for some reason, I was inspired by options beyond going back to sleep. I could get dressed and get out for a walk. I had time to get ready for the 8AM yoga class I never seemed to make. OR—I could get up and get over to the Horse Park where somebody was in trouble.

The Colorado Horse Park was, at the time, THE showgrounds for the area—at least in the hunter/jumper world. From leadline classes all the way up to the Grand Prix, it offered a multi-ring opportunity to learn, to grow and shine on those days when it all came together. But there were also those days when the wheels came off and it all came apart.

As I came up on a group of Winsome riders and trainers all gathered around a single competitor, Kato was the last horse I expected to see in that kind of trouble. Wound up, clearly. Eyes and nostrils wide, he had apparently just spooked his way around the entire course. They asked if I could try putting my hands on him—but clearly without any great expectations. Frankly, I had my doubts as well. We were in one of the busier, more congested areas of the whole park. It was at once a pathway linking most of the grounds, the most immediate holding area for competitors in going in one of the rings, the place where some of the courses were posted—and therefore a place for trainers to congregate with their clients for a final prep—a viewing area with a small stand for friends and family, and now apparently Reiki Central. Because Kato and his rider Shannon Gossman were on call for the next round, we needed to be right there.

I reached out and put my hand on his neck, then his shoulder, and finally right where both came together. It didn't really feel like the energy was going anywhere, but then slowly I could feel a glimmer of the young horse I had known before. Our breathing began to come into sync, and slow down. His head dropped a flinch. Then, of course, they were called for their next round. I did a quick Reiki "close" making sure he was on balance and stepped away.

Apparently, all the monsters and ghosts had now left the arena—or perhaps Kato, "Kensington Ask" in the ring, was now equal to them. He sailed around the course with something very much like his usual aplomb. I worked on him a few more times as he went in and out of the ring. Shannon joked that I was hired, but the truth was Kato had allowed me to learn twice. The first time in the stall in the first day of my equine Reiki journey, and then that Reiki could work any place and any time—no matter how hectic. For these lessons, I am grateful.

Still, I wanted to know more. I was beginning to have the sense that horses were healing me every bit as much as I was healing them. Luckily, Colorado—and the West—was ground zero for a different way to look at horses.

[Chapter 16]

> *"Animals were once, for all of us, teachers.*
> *They instructed us in ways of being and perceiving*
> *that extended our imaginations,*
> *that were models for additional possibilities."*
> *~ Joan McIntyre*

Devon Combs: A Conversation

We all approach our dreams from different paths. Some are perfect for the timid, some are adventurous, some tenuous, and some downright hellbent. But who's to say which path will get you through?

For Devon Combs, where she started was where she would finally come home. It was just a "hella" long way around. Dev is wonderfully articulate, so I'll let her tell her own story, as she told it to me.

DC: "I grew up with horses. So...my parents both had horses. And we did have a little pony. When I was a little girl, I remember riding every Sunday with them. And I didn't *love* it at the time. It was just something I did with my family. But it wasn't until I was ten and the other girls in school started taking riding lessons and I started taking riding lessons with them, and for some reason then something clicked. I become *obsessed* with horses. It became my lifestyle and my identity.

MH: Ah! And what kind of identity?

DC: Horse girl. Barn girl.

MH: OK.

DC: The girl wearing riding boots to school. The girl who only talked about horses. It felt like a comfortable fit for me. And the older I got I really leaned into that identity, especially in middle-school and high school when everybody seemed to gravitate toward different things. The "horse girl" reputation and identity was my foundation.

If you're lucky, and many of us used to be, there's a kind of innocence that rules early childhood. Confident in, confident of, the demi-gods of our world—parents, teachers, besties, and of course our beloved keepers of the animal kingdom— we venture forth. Exploring. Learning. Testing. Dreaming. Making mistakes. Innocent of judgment for whatever time the world allows. But for all of us, it pretty much finally crashes down in a single event.

High school. Hormones rage. What was once clear and certain, fades. But worse, that sense of knowing oneself, that certainty wobbles. And for many, it will be years before that "knowing", that second innocence, can be found again...

DC: It was late high school, that my mom went on a crazy diet. She'd always been a dieter, but she went on a really intense diet...and I had prom coming up. And I thought I'd try the diet too. I ended up dropping a ton of weight, really quickly, in about five weeks. It was a liquid diet. And for the first time in my life, I started getting all this outside attention. So, people say, "God, you look great...you're just beautiful!" And it really got its hooks in me. And I became really attached to external validation. I thought something was wrong with me before. Nobody'd ever said those things. So, it—external validation—became my new high. Made me feel special. Made me feel powerful. Pretty. But physically I was starving. So, Prom Night I remember binging my face off in the bathroom and then eating solid food for the first time in five weeks. And that's where it started; I couldn't stop. The binging and purging became my new foundation.

A long, hard descent begins. And worse, her one true supporter, her forgotten best friend would be left behind.

DC And right at the time I was about to leave for college...and I *sold my horse*...and that really made a big impression, because I didn't have my safety net. And I went to college thinking I was done with the horse world, and I was going to become this beautiful, skinny, surfing chick...

MH: Where'd you go to college?

DC: UC Santa Barbara

MH: Was it nice?

DC: It was a beautiful place; the dorm was on the beach. And eating got out of control. I didn't know how to express my feelings. I felt this huge external pressure to fit in. And I was suffering in silence. I was miserable.

MH: So how long did you try to keep going with that? Without help.

DC: Four years. I didn't know how to ask for help. I was raised in a family that never asked for help. We always had a smile on our face and hid all our feelings that weren't uplifting.

Well, I ended up dropping out of Santa Barbara, because I was binging and purging seven times a day. I couldn't make class.

MH: Jesus!

DC: Yeah...so *(laughs a bit)* I came home...showed up at my parents' doorstep. I had dropped out of school...packed up my car with all my dorm stuff. And they knew something was wrong, but I couldn't articulate it. So, I changed schools. I ended up at CSU. But again, you can't outrun an addiction. So, I joined the polo team at CSU, thinking that if I was with horses again, I'd be ok. I was joining the horse world kind of like my eating disorder. It was very much "control", ego-based. It was about performance. And that didn't do it. I was still suffering, and I didn't tell a soul. Nobody knew. I didn't tell *a soul*. But then I thought, well hell, maybe I really need to get away, and I thought maybe running away to New Zealand would help. So, I moved to New Zealand. I got a holiday visa, thinking that if I'm halfway round the world, maybe I can leave this struggle behind. And in turn, it got even worse down there. I really struggled. And I even worked at a horse farm down there thinking that if I'm back with horses...but it was a different relation to horses down there. It was the one-way street horse relationship. And it was back in the performance world where it was about "doing" not "being" with horses. There was no heart connection with the horse...

MH: Did you have a heart connection with your horse?

DC: I wasn't able to articulate it at the time. It was always after the show, sitting in the barn with the horses, listening to the horses eating hay, when I felt most connected

61

to them and to myself. Where I didn't have to put on a façade. I didn't have to be in control. I didn't have to worry about how I looked. I could just be.

MH: I know you reached a nadir. Can you talk about it a bit? The point of no return.

DC: Yeah, the point of no return. I left New Zealand; I came home with my tail between my legs. I was a failure. I couldn't figure this out. I couldn't get my life together. I was 21 at the time. Everyone around me looking happy and bouncing around. But I just felt so much pain. And I ended up trying to harm myself.

I went from the hospital where my parents had to put me, because I was overdosing on sleeping pills, to a psych ward where they put me on anti-depressants, and that didn't help. So, then they put me in a treatment center in Arizona. And that's where my healing started. But the point of no return really started when I came home from New Zealand. The shame. Not knowing who I was. Happy-go-lucky horse-loving girl had disappeared. I didn't know who I was anymore. I couldn't find her again. It turned out I wasn't meant to find her through the competitive show world of horses, I was meant to find her through the heart connection with horses. And that I discovered in Arizona, in a treatment center called "Mirasol," which changed my life.

MH: Was there a particular horse there?

DC: Yeah. So, this is how this went. There were ten women in the treatment center, all struggling with different disorders.

There were all kinds of different women there: 80 lbs. 350 lbs. They put bulimics, anorexics, compulsive over-exercisers, and compulsive overeaters together, which was powerful, because we all had to work through triggers. We all triggered each other.

MH: God!

DC: But this treatment center was holistic. I didn't even know what that word meant at that time. Yoga, art therapy, reiki, all this stuff I'd never heard of in my 21 years. And they had equine therapy. And I remember being on the van where we drove to the equine therapist's farm. And we got out and walked through the barn and there were no saddles, no bridles. There was a round pen, with a horse *loose*. And Marla, the equine therapist, asked our group of ten women, "who wants to work with the horse first?" And my hand shot up. This was one area in my life...and in my heart...I knew I still had a connection with horses. And I was so excited to be back at a barn. And she said, great, Devon! And I want you to walk around in the round pen. Go be with Jack." I walked in, and this was one area where I still had confidence: I'm good with horses. So, I walked into the round pen, Mary, and this big, beautiful bay horse...his name was Jack...he saw me coming and I'm walking toward him. He looked at me...turned his butt to me...and walked as far away from me as he could get.

MH: My God...

DC: And this was with ten people watching. I remember feeling mortified, humiliated, and like, a loser, like a failure, all the other things my ego was chirping at in my life. I truly felt like a total fuckup. Even the horse didn't want to be with me at that point. And the therapist from the outside of the round pen, said, "Devon, I want you to stop. Stop. Stop trying so hard. Close your eyes, stand still. And breathe. And I did what she said, and I remember with my eyes closed she led me through a grounding meditation. And suddenly, this wave of emotion started to come up. And for the first time in my life, I could not stop it. And I remember starting to wail. It's like this wall came down. And all the tears and fears I'd had my entire life started to come through. And come out. And I couldn't control it. And in that moment that horse Jack, from the farthest part of the round pen, turned around, looked right at me, and as I was sobbing in the middle of this round pen, he walked right up to me and put his nose to my heart. And he didn't move. I remember feeling this wave of compassion coming from him that I'd never felt before. And I looked into his eyes and this horse had nothing but pure love and acceptance. He did not move. And I was a sobbing mess. I put my arms around his neck; I was crying into his mane—he had tears streaked all over his mane—but this sweet horse did not move. He stood with me in my deepest pain, and it changed my life. Because in that moment I realized, I've had this all wrong. I thought if people saw who I truly was, imperfect, messy, not having my shit together, that they would run for the hills. And this horse did just the opposite. That's when he wanted to be with me. When I was being *real* ...and authentic.

And I'll never forget it. The light bulb went off that it's ok (little laugh) it's ok to be myself, I am ok as I am...and honestly, Mary, I knew. In that moment, I knew this calling...that I wanted people to have this kind of experience with horses, because it changed me forever. And going back on the van ride that day to the treatment center, for the first time I had hope...and excitement with my life...that this was why I grew up with horses...this was why I went and battled my own demons. This was why I came to this treatment center. It all made sense, because I have a greater purpose and it's to introduce people to THIS way of being with horses. It's not about control. It's not about your head, or the ego. It's about dropping below your neck, into your heart, and experiencing true authentic connection. That's when my healing happened and that's when my life changed. And I knew without a shadow of a doubt I was put in that position to help other people have a similar experience with horses.

MH: *I've been crying for the last five minutes, as I always do around Devon. I've joked that she broke me as I cry so readily now, but the truth is there is healing in these cracks and fissures. To quote Leonard Cohen, among others...." that's how the light gets in."*

[Chapter 17]

A Moment: The Power; The Blessing of a Horse

Talk to almost any horsewoman or man, and they will say the same thing. For all the excitement of a great round, for all the grace of a near perfect test, for all the joy of riding cross country or simply the surprise of jumping across a creek with your arse barely in the saddle but by damn still there, there is one moment that always offers the true promise of a horse.

The evening gathers in. You sit on a hay bale or trunk. Boots off, cleaned, and set aside. The scents linger. The leather cleaner. The hay. And the horses themselves, clean and tucked up for the night. For better or worse, the day is done. And the day's work is done too. Fed, watered and content, the horses are winding down as is every sound they make.

They breathe—and you hear them. And your own breath echoes. Tails twitch and you hear that too. This has always been their blessing—and yours. Knowing that this simple breathing quiet has the power to restore your soul. And heal your life—at least for this day.

[Chapter 18]

The Unbridled Workshop

A two-day retreat workshop for women to discover/rediscover who they meant to be. Who they are. And who they might still become. In the company of horses.

It sounded about right.

It was scheduled for my birthday weekend, and adding in horses, of course I figured this workshop was meant to be for me. A slam dunk. Just the thing. But not without some doubt. Some calls. And finally, one "verging on panic" question.

"I don't know what I'll be comfortable with. Is ok if I just listen?"

I'm pretty sure this wasn't the first time Devon Combs had been asked this in her years of leading workshops. I'm guessing folks who are seeking some sort of truth about their lives, often introspective souls, are not easily going to bare the same.

But after speaking with friends who knew Devon and the process, I was reasonably certain this was a good idea. Or at least worth a try. Couldn't hurt. At least not much.

One doesn't always see the good tears coming...

September 12-13. 2015:
The Unbridled Workshop

After a brief "getting to know you", the work began. Devon had four horses available to her on the property. Her own Detail, an appendix, and her alpha Playboy, a Rocky Mountain gaited horse. Also, Archer, the property owner's retired Thoroughbred and a Morgan mare named Blue, who boarded there. As I was to learn across this branch of the horse world, they each had their own gifts, strengths, and way of tuning into exactly who needed them.

I no longer remember exactly how the stories played out for others—which is just as well as they all remain in the gift of silence pledged in the opening of the weekend. No personal stories were to leave the arena—save your own, in your own heart. But there were exercises to open things up, many with your eyes closed but your senses starting to open.

We began in a circle. Tossing around a toy horse as we each, in our turn, began to speak. Why we were there; what we hoped for. For the brave: a telling of what was feared... or perhaps the hopes...even more brave?

A deck of cards had also been passed around, each person choosing their card by the picture on the back. These were Melisa Pearce's *"Whispers From A Horse's Heart."* I chose a horse who seemed to be exploding out into space, with every harness trace kicked away. While

I felt certain this would be about energy, the title of the card was clearing. And that would be the heart of my weekend's journey—ready or not.

At the core of the work, each person would sit with Devon and talk through their strongest concerns, worries, demons even. The chairs were just outside a round pen with one of the horses inside. (A round pen is one of the basics of horsemanship, often set up inside the arena.) We were all listening, even, and especially, the horse. As I focused in, my heart began to open to these lovely, fragile, strong, beleaguered, and enduring women, each with their own story. Sometimes Devon reflected the story back to them so they could hear what they were truly saying.

And sometimes the mirror was an entirely different being.

I had heard about the pantomiming, that horses—having picked up on the story—might then act it out giving the telling an entirely different perspective. I had heard about it but wasn't ready to buy into it yet. I mean it is, or it seems one of the more far-fetched aspects of the whole equine gestalt coaching thing...

But once it's right in front of you, it's a little harder to deny.

Convinced she had banished the demons from her past, one of the women was ready to press forward to new goals, and new paths to follow to get there. Declaring that she was ready to start, she opened the gate to the pen. She was paired with one of the larger horses, which made the pantomime all the more dramatic—once it started. Unencumbered, the horse was free to go anywhere in the arena and he did. As the client went in, the horse was gently but firmly moving away. She looked a little bewildered and you could see she wondered if she was rejected. Facing away from her, the gelding lay down—but not in any relaxed way. It was clear that he was holding a great deal of tension, almost folding himself into the smallest space possible. Then he looked back over his shoulder, fiercely not looking ahead—but looking straight at her. If you know horses, or even if you don't, it was easy to see this was not a comfortable position nor one that would be assumed without cause. So, his message was clear. In no way, shape or form had she released the past. Until this moment. The veneer cracked, and she then was sobbing with her whole heart. As these tears finally began to wash the past away, her horse partner stood and came to her, offering comfort and at long last—clarity.

Pantomime, while maybe the most dramatic, was not the only tool the horses used over the course of the day. Sometimes the women had faced a truth in talking to Dev outside the round pen and now only needed the deep-hearted comfort of a horse aligned to their chakras and synchronized to their breath to help lock in the lesson.

And then there were those who were wobbling be-
twixt and between, who had glimpsed a possible future—
for a moment—but didn't quite know if they were ready.
Sometimes Dev would add a ground pole that bisected
the arena. Where they were standing was where they
were—and that possible future was over there on the
other side of the pole. There was no judgment and no
pressure. There was, however, a horse. Standing beside
them for comfort—and perhaps courage. And then
choosing to stand behind them. Even now I imagine I
feel what they must have felt. The calm as they were
embraced by the energy field of the horse's heart. Then
the warm soft breath in the small of their back. And the
ever so gentle, and firm, push that was the horse letting
them know they were ready.

There are so many ways that one is brought to tears in
these retreats that I gave up trying to block them. I joke
now that Devon broke me, and I was no longer the stalwart, iron-willed person I once had been. And soon I
would learn that that was the best possible thing that
could have happened.

At the end of the first day, someone was still waiting
for me.

Seymour. My beloved. The Mighty. The horse that
was waiting for his grain and supplements. Luckily, he
was on my way home, not that it would have really mattered. He was the exact answer to this late afternoon, as
always—and he was ready. Touching his muzzle to my
heart and shoulder and back again. To my heart and

hand. Even after his evening ration of Senior feed and Aspireze 3, I thought I was just all revved up and that seeing what I had seen at Dev's was starting to color everything.

I had no idea.

The next day, I finally took my turn in the focus of the group. Dev asked and I began to talk—about all the hard losses and hard times. About the fear that once again almost consumed me most days now.

And about the days, way back in time, when I thought I knew who I was. Even though my horse was a pony and was 300 miles away most of the time—and shared by at least 20 other cousins, he was still a Champion—and I thought that made me a cowgirl. After all, I had the outfit, and wore it as many days as I was allowed. A fringed skirt and a fringed vest. Boots. And almost as importantly, a gun belt complete with cap guns. It wasn't that I wanted to shoot anything, I absolutely didn't—it was the swagger. It was 1950's TV with Dale Evans, and Annie Oakley.

Now, I felt like a pretender. An imposter. Even though I had worn my grown-up fringe jacket on this, my birthday, I still felt completely inauthentic. There may have been only one horse there that day who could break through my self-imposed blinkers.

Playboy. A Rocky Mountain gaited horse. Small but mighty. The alpha of this herd. And the one who was waiting for me—not in the round pen—but out in the arena. Because in a change of pace in this last session of the day, I was going to swing my blue-jeaned leg over his bare back, grab the halter's lead rope and mane—and ride.

Well, it wasn't quite as dramatic as that in the end. The shorter Playboy was considerably rounder than my own See, and there was definitely a bit of shoving involved in getting that leg across. But once there and with a deep breath, I was home. Maybe not forever. But in this moment...

It had been a powerful weekend, and I was a bit tired. More than. Maybe more wrung out, but exultant. Seeing however incompletely what could be. What horses could be. What they actually...maybe...are. Maybe what I could be. And maybe what I actually am. It was a vision to taunt, to suggest, to haunt, to hope but certainly to follow up on with another sweet, glorious morning.

Or so I thought.

Stopping off on the way home, I'd brought Seymour in to feed him his Senior mix. There were days, and this was one, when I would lean in close, scenting his contentment. Breathing it in. Hearing it too. Holding his bucket right next to my heart, while he munched away.

Still, I was tired as I took him back out to his pasture, slipped off his halter and started back towards the gate. He was coming behind me. Not unusual. But this was.

The breath. Blowing on the back of my head. Gentle. Focused. Intentional. I stood, arrested, knowing this was something out of the ordinary, even for the never ordinary Mighty. I turned and finally saw him for who he truly was, for he had dropped all pretense of anything else. It was like looking into the eyes of an ancient Zen Master. It was a vision that changed everything—though not straightaway.

Here's the thing I realized as time went by. All horses hide themselves away unless they're lucky enough to have born into a place that honors them as they are instead of for how we wish them to be. I'm not saying we don't get to wish or even ask for certain things from them; it's all in how. But if we're attentive, and compassionate, and gentle—and maybe just plain lucky, we might be gifted with this vision of who they truly are.

This was now a key to my quest.

[Chapter 19]

Giving Back. Clearing a Horse

Sometimes a horse will hold onto energy that's not necessarily good for them. They are intuitive geniuses at clearing old patterns from clients or even friends, but in doing so sometimes take it on themselves.

Detail, Devon Combs' beautiful Appendix mare, taught me this when I worked on her. We worked loose in the arena as "Deets" and I had a good understanding with her coming and going as she wished. On this particular day she kept offering her throat chakra. For people, that's usually about blocking things that need to be expressed. Sometimes it's just something that needs to be said out loud, even if there's no one to hear it beyond me and them. I explored that with her, trying to see if expressing something, or even if just acknowledging the need allowed the energy block to clear. It didn't. I finally realized she didn't feel like she had permission to let it go—and that it wasn't her "stuff" to begin with. This sweet girl was holding onto the energy that had been released by Devon's clients because she thought she should. Understand—as I came to—that Deets was very proud of the work that she did for Devon and her clients, and she worried that in letting go she might somehow fail them. I gave her permission to let go and then more importantly got Dev to tell her as well. At once the block eased, and the lesson was learned.

But it's not only therapy horses that hold on. Once when I was working on a friend's horse, Poppy, I came across a big energy block in her right rear hock. The Ki or Chi was flowing out of her hindquarters, specifically her right hip but came to a complete halt before I got very much farther down. I usually work my way in slowly, particularly with horses that are sensitive to energy. But she kicked out a little as if I had touched a tender place. I glanced up at Elizabeth Lord, her owner. She said Poppy was the same with the vet and the farrier although nothing was really wrong there. I remembered that Poppy had gotten cast (stuck on the ground under something) at a new barn and asked but no, Popstar—as we called her—had been healed some time before. It stuck with me though and I began to explore energetically. I could feel that sense of being trapped underneath something—in her case the pipe dividers between the stall runs. Was there some way that injuries persisted that weren't physical? Something horses could perceive but we couldn't, unless we really tried to tune in? Suddenly I could feel her "energy" body stretching some distance out from her skin. When I first felt this, I called it her ghost body, which in a way it was. Poppy had energetic memories of being cast that were still haunting her, hurting her—and they needed to be released. I did my best and things seemed better. Still, I checked in the next day. Elizabeth said Poppy had been really tired the night before, and slow to "wake" up the next day—but that when she did, she was moving beautifully! It always does my heart good to hear that, especially when we're talking about a lady in her 20s—in horse years! While what it that might be exactly in human years is always good for an energetic debate, there's no doubt Poppy was a senior citizen.

Once they know you're listening, horses really like to offer advice on how you could help their friends too. I had put Seymour away in the pasture and was headed back to the barn when I was presented with a picture of See's friend Al, uneasy and unbalanced. I turned to look back and of course, there was Seymour, looking at me. It had taken me a while to recognize these were messages, but I got this one loud and clear. Al was in the barn sedated from a dental procedure. Jane Cyphers, Al's person, was with him to make sure he stayed safe. But I realized a horse sedation was much like opening for a Reiki treatment, but while normally a horse can and does close itself, the drugs changed that. Al needed to be closed. Thanking See for the assist, I headed into the barn. Visualizing Al's energy knitting itself back together, I waved my hands up his back. With a deep sigh, he thanked me.

I love this work...

[Chapter 20]

Seymour Reikis A Rider

It was late one afternoon. The daytime riders had finished and headed home, and the evening folks were yet to come. A perfect time for me to be with See loose in the arena. I tried to do this a couple of times a week, telling myself we were working on our connection and communication, but the head groom/horse magician came closer to the truth.

"You going to play with your boy today?" He would always be smiling when he said it. I think he approved.

So yes, I was playing with Seymour, letting him stretch his legs and get out the kinks. While I didn't have the fitness of the unique equestrian Tik Maynard, I would sometimes trot over a few poles with him. But mainly I would walk with him, quietly, and sometimes with his muzzle on my shoulder. And we would breathe together. Most of the time I would follow his breathing; sometimes we fell into a natural sync.

Inevitably, eventually someone would call out "door", and I would catch See and answer. "Come Ahead." If they were looking to do serious work we would usually finish for the day, but sometimes it was another rider or two who just wanted to relax with their horse too. Maybe they just had a bridle on, or perhaps, like me, they sometimes tied the loose end of their lead rope up to the halter and mounted. We had really tall mounting blocks, so you could just lean over your horse's back and then swing a leg around. Although he was a warmblood, See did not have quite the girth of a Playboy—the fabulous other Reiki Master and part-time, gaited couch. So I was able to get on my own.

I don't know why it took me so long to hop on him bareback. I think I just no longer considered myself to be an immortal. But the thing is, it took me straight back. Just the feel of it, of being more attuned to your horse. And more free. Never even questioning where my leg was or my hands, never doubting that I was one with my horse, I just was.

And now, we were about to embark on another, quite different adventure. But still surprisingly as one. This time the rider at the door was alone. Not even her horse was with her. And she was limping in a twisted sort of way. As an extreme athlete, she was used to playing hurt. But this did not look good. Most of the people in the barn now knew I was a Reiki Practitioner and she was no exception. Still.

She asked if I could Reiki her, then and there. No table, no chair. Just a friend in pain, in the middle of an arena. I had no idea how to even go about it but had to try. I tried to visualize the table turned and stood on its end. She stood with her back to me. See was still loose in the arena. She asked if we should put him away, but I was beginning to get an inkling of what might be possible. No assumptions. No restrictions. Just possibility. I said, I think he'll be fine. Let's see what happens.

I started by balancing the chakras from the back, working my way down from the top. As I got to the heart chakra, See came and stood in front of her, perpendicular to us but with his heart chakra aligned. The energy lifted and then began to flow back and forth between See and me —and through her. I could hear a thrumming sound like a giant engine coming up to speed.

And then I could feel it. This sweep of energy moving back and forth, powerful, healing heart to heart to heart. Back and forth, like an electrical surge. As that finally slowed down, See came around and put his muzzle in the crook of my neck, still supporting the energy, but delicately now. The energy lifted, and finally lifted away. More than a little uncertain, I asked her how she was doing, how she was feeling. She said, "How about if I just show you?"

And she walked away. Perfectly. No cramped back. No terribly foreshortened stride. No tight joints. None of it.

She was well. And she was whole.

I was amazed. And Seymour was still right there beside me, his muzzle in that place that I've come to believe symbolizes—and is—total trust. Faith. A connection with no filters.

Perfect, really, as a symbol or more a sign of what this connection can be.

[Chapter 21]

Again and Again, Long-Distance Reiki

It was a Sunday evening, and I was sitting out in my sunroom/Reiki studio in Castle Rock, CO. This had been a lovely weekend with no deadlines looming over my head. My sister and I have a writing company, and in those days, we got a lot of last-minute assignments, almost always it seemed on Friday for a Monday delivery. All things considered, I was not inclined to get up and go find the phone when it rang.

But it was a friend, a very good friend in fact, Kathleen. We met in our high school French class at the NC School of the Arts, so long time friends as well.

She has a daughter, Jessie, who is very medically involved. After an age of trying to care for her at home, my friend had finally managed to get her into a superb care situation, The Center for Discovery in Monticello, NY.

A few months before this call, we had decided to try Long-Distance Reiki with Jessie to see if it could help. Long-Distance had become a specialty of mine, so I was hopeful, but I had never worked with someone like this before. While Jess was a joyful maker of a wide range of sounds, she is non-verbal. Kath and I settled on a plan.

She would be in the room with her daughter and the phone on speaker, and I would have my phone on speaker too. That way Kathy could let me know if there were any unusual reactions, and then I could modify what I was doing. So we began, I up in my writing room on the top floor of my house and Kath and Jess in her room at the Center. I tried sending energy to all the places in her body where I knew she had issues, but finally settled on being very still and letting the energy go where it would.

With any long-distance session, I go until I can feel the energy in my hands winding down. As it did, I reached out to Kath to let her know I was wrapping it up. But as it turned out, Jessie wasn't quite ready to let go yet. She wanted to "talk" to me. Whereupon this glorious flow of sound, joyous and unfettered, swept through my phone. Without pausing for sentences or words or even syllables, because there were no words, Jessie let me know she was grateful. Happy. And that she felt good. I was moved. And touched. And of course, I was crying.

So when this call for a second session came, I was up for it with no hesitation. The first session was done in concert with her initial Botox shot, which had been successful. In direct opposition to the normal effect, successful Botox for Jess meant greater freedom of movement, some release and relief from the spasms that would lock her up. Tellingly, her second Botox shot was less successful, and the doctors were reluctant to try again. But Kathy, being the mama tigress health warrior who had protected her child for so long, was having none of it. She finally convinced them to try again, and on this Sunday evening she had been told it would be administered the next day. At 9 o'clock, her time, as I understood it. 7 AM for me. Was I up for it? But of course. Kath rang off saying she'd be back in touch with more details.

And immediately another voice was in my ear. Now, I don't claim to be an animal communicator. For the most part, I just don't have that certainty that I'm actually talking to a separate being. Save for one. Seymour was not only able to make himself heard, but often he was clear and "talking" at a breakneck pace.

Mary, I need to be there. I need to be a part of this. Jessie needs me. You need me. She knows. Let me be there.

Still, it was always a surprise, if not an outright shock, to hear him. Also, it was hard to know what he meant. What there? Did he want me to be out in the pasture with him at 7A? Somehow, I was sure that the Henry family, who lived on the farm, would be less than charmed that I was showing up in their pasture that early. As I puzzled, Kathy called back and I tried to figure out how to broach it to her.

"Did Jessie ever have a special connection to horses, or a particular horse? Cause Seymour seems to think he has a part to play here. "

She couldn't think of anything, so we went back to sorting the details. I would tune into Jessie at 7AM and stay connected until a text or call released me.

I was given the address, always important with long distance work, and began to work on the simple details. 7AM was not primetime for me, so some earlier alarms would be needed. I find it helps to have a picture to focus on and printed one where the joyful part of Jessie's nature was in full bloom.

Suddenly, Kathy was calling me back with her heart in her throat.

"Daisy. She loved Daisy when she was really young. In Germany!"

Slowing down, she explained that Jessie had been treated with Hippotherapy when she was a young child in Germany. Hippotherapy, especially for the young, had been found to be particularly effective with children with her issues. Now, my beautiful German guy had sussed that out and realized she needed him. After many tears we had agreed there would be a way. And that we would figure it out. Or he would.

The next morning, I wasn't so sure, but I was hopeful. I also had no idea how to pull this together. I'd never tried a multi-channel long-distance treatment before. With so many involved, I decided to not use the cellphone, but to rely on my intuition instead. Now with pictures printed out of Seymour, Jessie and her address spread around my quilt, I was ready to try. I offered the invitation to See to come, blessed and then opened the "channel" to Jessie. I could feel a lot of good energy, but no special connection to Seymour yet. With a long-distance treatment, I do track time so that I can correlate what anyone else saw or felt. Around 7:40 AM my time, I could feel the energy starting to shift, build—and off in the distance the faint sounds of hooves. He was coming. Hoofbeats became a thundering gallop. And then See was there. Without a pause, as always in stride, he lifted up into his perfect, fancy jump, cleared my right shoulder and cantered off down into the channel.

To say it was one of the more moving, exhilarating, and sacred moments of my life is an understatement.

Also, it wasn't over yet.

When I felt the energy was done, I closed the channel , took a deep breath, and called Kathy.

"Did anything special happen around 9:40 or so?"

"They decided everything was ready and that they would start the treatment early."

Turns out I had misheard. The prep for the treatment, which was elaborate, would start at nine. The treatment itself was scheduled for 10. Only they decided around 9:40 to go ahead...

He knew.

Again, contrary to the cosmetic applications, they can't measure the response to the process right away. It can take days or even a week to fully assess how effective a treatment had been.

But three days later, there was this....

Jess. Pedaling on her cycle trainer. Not perfect. Having to really work to get the pedal over the top so she could press down again. Imperfect. Save for this. She had never been able to do that before. Or even anything close. And is that not our heart's measure for success?

[Chapter 22]

A Conversation with Ann Baldwin

Even in and of itself, the sheer volume and weight of anecdotal proof should really convince us about horses and their full-on gift of healing. By now, it seems as if everyone knows someone who's experienced the transformative kindness, or the power of the unflinching authenticity, or even just the depth of a creature who stands beside you and does not back away. The generosity that allows you to fling your arms around their neck and sob until your heart finally stills—and runs clean.

But I want to honor this truth, and so have kept looking to science for a proof.

Luckily, I wasn't alone. A far more competent person was also looking for answers—and from a strikingly broad perspective. I was lucky enough to do a phone interview, and her answers were so fluent I've kept them largely intact.

Ann Baldwin, PhD, Physiology; Masters in Radiation Physics; Bachelor's degree in Physics, was doing research at NIH when her career took an unexpected turn...

AB: I was doing experiments on rats, and I could see the rats were getting stressed. And at that time, I needed someone to help me analyze data. So I hired this woman who had done Reiki—I'd never heard of Reiki before— and she suggested we try using it on the rats. And I saw that it worked on the rats, so I gradually got more interested in it. So, it's kind of weird how it just suddenly appeared.

AB: (Laughs) And then she did an attunement on me. And I also had a student and a post-doc in my lab.

MH: And how did they respond to it. I mean...is there the skepticism that one might imagine, or are people more open to it?

AB: Oh! A high degree of skepticism. In fact, as a result, I gave up my tenured position at the university... because I just got so humiliated by people's comments.

MH: So, was that at the University of...Arizona?

AB: So now I'm still at the university, but I work part-time. My position is different. But yes, I was a full-time researcher, and when I switched to this kind of work people thought I wasn't a real scientist anymore. As I said, NIH is not funding Reiki. They were once: I got a grant...but they haven't for many years. The info on their website is disgusting. I mean it's just totally inaccurate what they have up there.

MH: About Reiki?

AB: Yes. I've confronted them about it, but nothing has changed."

Still, Ann was undeterred—or largely so. For the last 15+ years, she has focused on stress reduction—again with some surprising partners.

AB: I've gotten more and more interested in horse-human reactions. I'm doing experiments now with both horses and humans and making measurements on both as they interact in special ways.

I've done three phases of this experiment. We're looking at older people—55+. In the first one they interacted with horses by tuning into the horses' energy fields with their hands. We measured heart rate variability of the horses and the humans as they did that. And we found that—we had 24 people in this study—and we found that the people's heart rates significantly increased, which is good. Because heart rate variability is a measure of the ability of your heart to adjust to your needs. So that went up. And then the horses...their heart rates vary, or oscillate, at a very low frequency. And we found that at this very low frequency, we were starting to see the same result in the humans later on. After or during the interaction. The humans were shifting to this very same frequency as the horses.

I found a few studies that show that this particular range of frequencies of heart rate variability, if people don't have much of it, they're more prone to PTSD and inflammation. So having more of it is good. It seemed that interacting with horses in this way was giving the people more of this frequency in their hearts. And then, we did another one where they were grooming the horses and we saw a similar effect. And then we've just done another one, with Linda Kohanov[5], actually, with an exercise called "rock back and sigh" where they walk towards the horse and if they see the horse acknowledging their presence, like moving their ears, or looking at them, then they rock back and sigh to relieve tension and relax. And then they go closer to the horse. And we did the same thing there. We're analyzing that data now.

And we measured self-esteem in people; self-esteem significantly improved in humans after the interaction with the horse. But in all these three types of interactions, we noticed the same thing, in heart rate variability in people: heart rate increasing in people and also the shift in people toward the horse's very low frequency.

MH *I'm not ashamed to admit that my head was starting to spin a little, not only from trying to master the details of what she was saying but the enormity of what all this could mean. I wanted to be very clear, so I asked if she could explain it one more time.*

AB: I understand. It's tricky to get. Most people think that if you're just sitting there, that your heart rate should just stay the same. But it doesn't. It varies. It changes even if you're just sitting there. And the more it changes, the healthier you are. Because it means your heart is able to adjust very quickly according to our needs. And if you're stressed, you tend to have reduced heart-rate variability. It's not changing very much. There's not a balance. Heart-rate variability is produced by a balance between the sympathetic and the parasympathetic nervous systems. Sympathetic increases it. Parasympathetic decreases it. Like the accelerator and the brake on a car. And if you've got the accelerator on all the time like the sympathetic component, you're just going to have the heart rate beating fast and it won't vary much. It's like your foot's always on the accelerator. And if your foot's always on the brake, it's like your parasympathetic component's always on, and the heart rate is low. And it never changes, and you feel tired. And the best thing is to have a balance between the two, so the heart rate goes up and the parasympathetic brings it down. And then the sympathetic brings it up again. So it oscillates. And that's what heart rate variability is. And the more of that you have the healthier you are. And it's very good because it can show you how stressed a person or an animal is.

MH: We often talk about energy fields... around animals, whatever? Has that been proven?

AB: Oh, yes. The brain produces a small field, and the heart produces a large field. And they can be measured using expensive instruments called SQUIDs—"superconducting quantum interference device.[6] I did an experiment on one actually. And you're able to measure the field – the field is very weak that the heart produces, but it's quite extensive. It can stretch out as far as 12-15 feet from the person. And also the fields...they have an oscillation. So the heart rate oscillates; it doesn't just stay the same. The healthier you are, the more it oscillates. And if you're really healthy and in tune, it oscillates at a particular frequency. And that oscillation is also seen in the heart fields; it pulses with this frequency. So, yes, electromagnetic fields produced by people are real.

MH: Is there any research on animals producing the same?

AB: Have you read any of Linda Kohanov's work? She's written a few books and she has a ranch near where I live. And she has done programs for people from all over the world with horses. She discovered that the energy fields of horses have layers. And you can teach people— I've done it, and you can probably do it too, to feel these layers of energy fields. As you get closer to the horse you can feel another layer with your hands. You can knock on the layer, and they'll look at you. The electromagnetic fields are produced by anything with a heart. In fact, horses' hearts are 4 x the size of humans, so...the field is probably stronger.

~

Challenge accepted. Many, many months later. But as I reviewed this work, I realized I hadn't tried this yet. Merida, one-time rescue, one-time Reiki "client", now my groundwork partner and the full-time heart hero for Charity N. Williams, seemed the perfect candidate. She is a sensitive mare—though she had been quite guarded, almost completely shut down when we first met at the rescue. She was there with her filly and an even younger colt. All had been abused in their own way and I couldn't help reaching out to them. She would come and lean against the gate while I worked on her. Soon the whole family would be there, crowding round to share energy. I would end up throwing a "blanket" of Reiki over them all. They reminded of nothing as much as huddled refugees yearning for their own place in the world. Merida found that place when she finally let the trainer Charity in and loved her. Now out in her own well-deserved place at a local farm, Merida was helping to teach me the ins and out of groundwork. So, one day while I was explaining this heart energy experiment to Charity, Merida was close by but quite occupied by watching the new horse in the adjacent paddock. I reached out to see if I could feel it and if Merida would respond. It was not a sudden movement and in no way unexpected for her—yet her head whipped around as I mentally "tapped."

I've tried it since with other horses and gotten the same response, though none quite as dramatic as hers. It's worth a try if you want to experiment too, and worth a thank you when they respond.

~

In the time between our interview and this book, Dr. Baldwin[9] has gone on to publish her work Effects of a Form of Equine-Facilitated Learning on Heart Rate Variability, Immune Function, and Self-Esteem in Older Adults with Barbara Rector and Ann Alden.

In addition, she is an advisor to students who are expanding on her work at the University of Arizona. After a long career researching into the mechanisms of macromolecular transport between blood and tissue, including in vivo testing of hemoglobin-based blood substitutes, her interests turned to the physiological effects of mental and emotional stress. She now quantitatively evaluates the effectiveness of various methods commonly used to reduce stress focusing on heart rate variability and peripheral blood flow as outcome parameters for autonomic function. Her studies include the use of equine-human interactions, Reiki, music, laughter yoga and heart focused breathing. She leads one of the few re-search teams in the world that studies synchronous changes in heart rate variability of horse-human pairs to determine whether physiological information is being transferred between species. Dr. Baldwin also serves as Editor-in-Chief for the Center of Reiki Research and maintains its curated webpage of all peer-reviewed, pub-lished, scientific research studies involving Reiki."

Linda Kohanov is possibly best-known for The Tao of Equus: A Woman's Journey of Healing & Transformation through the Way of the Horse, but several of her books are available at Amazon and other outlets.

[Chapter 23]

A Moment Connecting

I always wanted a true connection to nature. Honestly, I wanted to speak to it all. The animals, of course, the trees, the air but even more—I wanted to listen and to hear what they had to say. I wanted that validation, I suppose, that I was worthy of this. It took me a while, but I finally realized all you have to do is observe and to notice. They become aware that you're aware and little by little the conversation begins. It was only in my mind that worthiness had anything to do with it. Now, more and more often as I write this, the connection strengthens. Even when my old friend Doubt raises its unlovely head, it can be banished by the simplest of gestures—a glance out the window ...

They're back—the birds that is. Yesterday a robin calmly perched in the bushes across my family's narrow driveway, and then the young cardinal came. Beautiful and quite frisky, he couldn't show me enough perfect poses. The robin remained serene and steady throughout. Between the pair of them, I began to believe in my own calling again. This morning a house finch hovered just over my still hung Christmas lights fluttering like a hummingbird before heading off.

The final visitor was a butterfly, a yellow Monarch, I think. There are days when I truly want (ok, need) these winks from the universe—from nature. And blessèd be, they come.

[Chapter 24]

Melisa Pearce. Moving Towards Joy

A goodly portion of my gratitude in life is reserved for the horse people I met in Colorado; the ones who helped me find my way back to a deep attunement with nature. Many of them wouldn't, couldn't have, known, at least at first, that I was following along—that every post, every message they crafted so mattered to me. I was hungry, and this was divine sustenance. But truly...I didn't really know it yet either.

As always, and/or maybe just because I gave it so much attention, work led me to yet another key path. Jody Haas, connected through Denise Horton, was looking to create a television treatment for an idea she had. This idea had led her to the Rocky Mountain Horse Expo. She was looking to meet this cowboy horse whisperer, whose name I can't remember.

Instead, she met Melisa Pearce.

Which is another way of saying the divine has its own plan. After listening to Melisa's presentation, and talking to her afterward, Jody knew she'd found her true subject—but she wasn't sure how to move it forward. Her very good friend Denise suggested Jody might do well with a co-writer, editor, and all-around coach—and I was happy to be recommended. The divine may well have had its own plan for me, too.

I don't want to take too much credit—Jody had and still has a wonderful vision for a show that would celebrate horses as healers—and Melisa and her healing herd. But the work together was a wonderful step forward for me into my own destiny.

I met Melisa Pearce several times over the course of that project and then in my own pursuit of what mattered to me. There was a From Fear to Love workshop where the Friday evening was open to the public. Even though it was a bit of a haul up to Boulder and back in an evening, I got to witness firsthand the behaviors that the horses used to bring insight into a story. I met Anna Twinney here too, an animal communicator who would play such "pivotal" a role in helping me understand Seymour on a whole new level when the time came.

When I began researching *Horse Heroes*, and the many ways horses work with us to heal, I knew I needed to interview this extraordinary woman. Luckily, she is as kind and generous as she is insightful.

Horses have been central in Melisa Pearce's life, one way or another, since she was a child. They served as her escape, her friends, comforters, listeners and eventually teachers and healers. While this sounds dangerously like every other horse-mad girl, hers is one of the profoundly transforma-

tional stories of horses as healers, and she is now one of their truest, most grounded advocates.

Melisa is the owner of Touched by a Horse, Inc, and Founder of the Equine Gestalt coaching program, as well as the Gestalt Coaching Method Certification Program. She is also a writer of the YA novel "Eponalisa, The Fall Ride" and several non-fiction books about horses. Divinely guided but not wholly protected, Melisa chose to walk a sacred path—with a lively sense of fun. But in the beginning, it was simply native to her.

MP: I had my first horse when I was ten years old and began trail riding, and then moved into showing. And I've actually owned a three-time world champion all-around stallion and done showing at the World and the Congress [7] and that kind of level. Reining was my passion, and I did that for many, many years. Concurrently with that, I became a psychotherapist and a coach, and then started this work with horses in the mid-80's.

M.H. I think I've heard the stories about how this started, but the one thing I wanted to ask you before that was, did they heal you before you recognized it as such?

M.P. Yes. That's a great question. To back up—my parents had a very turbulent, terrible marriage, so my horses were my confidantes, and they were where I ran to feel safe, and feel heard. So certainly, as a teenager I knew them as my healers and best friends before I even understood what that was. When I did my own personal therapy in my 20s, it was my horses that really kept me on the planet. And then after becoming a psychotherapist, and in the middle of showing horses and doing all of this, I just began to see them so differently. And with my private practice clients—I started combining my private practice clients and my retreat clients with the horses in the mid-80's—I saw it.

M.H. And did you get the sense that they recognized you before you recognized the possibilities in yourself?

M.P. Yes. I say sometimes to people, that I do feel that I was chosen, in a way, to bring this field of horse and human healing forward to the public because when I was doing it in the mid-80's, of course we did not have the luxury of the internet, or Google, or any of that, so there was no way to know if anyone else was doing it. And it was a good twenty years later that I found out Barbara Rector was in Tucson, I was in Flagstaff, you know; that there were others putting together some forms of therapy—and recognizing horses for that. But for me, I did feel like they were showing me something and they were saying, "Will you wake up to this? And will you bring it forward?" And I feel like I did kind of step up to the calling, I guess, and speak up on their behalf.

M.H. Could you talk about when you realized horses could be your co-practitioners? How you discovered it and then developed it?

M.P. Well, for me again, I didn't have any other model to look at, so I was developing my own. And I know that a lot of models have either two people working, or you know, just different ways of looking at it.

What I recognized was the horses were giving me information. I never conceptualized it in the first place, Mary, that the client would choose the horse, or that the horse would be somehow part of the game, I didn't even have the conception of Eagala,[8] or any of those other methods.

For me, my horses were directly giving me information around the client and the client's needs. I saw them as my co-coaches. I felt like what they were doing was so valuable, and so misunderstood by most people, that I could share that information with them about the client. Rather than seeing the horse working with the client, I really see that the horse is coaching the client and giving me a ton of information.

I've had some remarkable experiences like that. I had a mare not too long ago, when I was working with a family whose younger son has been in rehab for about six months, and their older son came with the mom and dad to the session. And we're doing a family work, so that they're in good shape when the younger son returns home. It was an all-day situation, and the father had done some deep personal work, the mother had done some deep personal work, and after lunch, it was going to be the son's turn.

We broke for lunch and came back, and I put this mare named Thirty-Thirty in the round pen with the son as I was asking him questions. But she stopped him, she pushed him up against—I've never seen her do it before—but pushed him, kind of with her muzzle up against the fence. His back was actually against the fence. And then she looked at me, and I thought, "Hmm, what are you doing? What are you showing me?" And she pushed on his chest, and then looked at him for a sec, then went over to the bars of the round pen and started running her teeth left and right on one of the bars, just like a monkey trying to get out of a cage; it was just bizarre. And I looked at her and I thought, "Thirty, what are you telling me?" And she went back over to him, looked at me, looked at him, and pushed his chest. And I finally got what she was saying to me, that it was a vice, there was something about a vice. It was the only way she could think to pantomime to me there's something not right, this person has a habit that's not right.

And I looked at him and said, "If I didn't know better, I would say my horse is busting you for being high right now." And he sunk to the ground and started crying. And what came out of the piece was: he's the one who turned his younger brother on to the drugs...

M.H. Oh, my God.

M.P. ... and got him in so much trouble. And he had never told the parents, and neither had the younger brother; it was the family secret. And there's the mare saying, "He's not okay. I can't work with him; I don't want to be in the ring with him because he's not okay." And that was her way of showing me in a pantomime, "Hey, this is what's happening with this guy."

It's things like that: she wasn't working with him, she was working with me about him, you know. And that's just one tiny example, but that's what they show me every day.

I had a women's retreat with ten women, and on Sunday morning, we were transitioning from doing the deep personal work to lighter stuff. And this tenth person had not done any personal work yet, but because I believe in contracting with the client, I said to her, "If it's not right for you, I totally respect that, and we can move on to something else. But I don't want to do that without asking you, do you want to do some personal work?" She said, "I absolutely do."

So, she came up to sit in the chair. She was 70 years old. And she said, "I don't know exactly what I'm going to work on." I said, "You don't have to know. Tell me a little bit about yourself."

While telling me a little bit about herself, she said she'd been a medical doctor, but she had relinquished her license. Well, that's not something you hear every day, and I knew that today she was a therapist. I said, "Can you tell me just a little bit of background around the decision to stop being a medical doctor?" And she said, "Well, I've really only shared this story with my sister, but I'll share it with you."

Next, we're speaking just outside the round pen—sitting in two chairs. Inside the round pen was a mare named Tory. I had had Tory since her birth, and she was just very wise around everything. Tory came over and just stood, looking like she was listening, like she was the third being in the conversation.

So, the woman, Diane, said, "I first graduated from medical school, I wanted to get married, have kids, have a family, all that life, but I didn't have that yet, when I got an opportunity to go to Africa, so I took it. I went to Africa as a doctor and this was many, many years ago, right? I was there at a time when they really needed the help. And I was scared, it was my first gig as a doctor, and I wasn't sure what I could do. And what I found was, they were amazingly poor in equipment and things that the people needed. It was a really challenging time, throughout the two-and-a-half years I stayed there. A lot of people were very, very ill and dying because the country was in a severe drought."

When Diane left Africa, her senior advisor said, "I'm really disappointed in you." And she said, "What? I've been here two-and-a-half years." He said, "Yeah, but you're going back to the States, and I thought you'd hang in there with us." So, she was kind of guilted about it. But she went back to the U.S. She went to work in a Seattle hospital as a physician; she worked there about five years. And that always bothered her, that her advisor had said that.

She still wasn't married, still didn't have kids, so she went back to Africa. But in the five years she'd been gone, the rains had come, and the drought was no longer there. So, people weren't starving to death any longer. Earlier in the story, she had gone into great detail about how they were starving to death, and how they buried their babies in the sand, and really a lot about those earlier years in Africa.

And then the second time she was there, she was a more senior physician sitting on a board of doctors from all over the world. She said, "None of us at that table, all very fine physicians, thought about the fact that something as simple as measles could come through there." And measles did come through there, and they had 14,000 deaths. After that, she said, "I just hung up my license. I thought, I'm not meant to do this, it's just too hard. I came back, re-trained to be a psychotherapist, and that's what I'm doing today."

Meanwhile, my mare is listening to all of this and she—the woman told the story in a much more graphic way than I'm telling it to you now, in much fuller detail. And nobody was without tears in their eyes, over hearing about those years in Africa, and what this woman had seen, and their sadness for the African people.

I asked the woman to stand in the middle—I asked them to stand in the middle of the pen—she was not a horseman. And my mare usually would approach people and kind of take a quick, you know, Reiki assessment, "How are they?"

M.P. But instead, this time, she went around the edge of the pen with her lip, moving it left/right, on the very edge of the 60-foot round pen. And I asked Dianne, "Do you know what she's doing by any chance?" And she said, "I think she's rejecting me." And I said, "Well, I believe my angel's working...my horse is working the angelic realm." I said, "I don't think they do anything negative, so I'm going to say, not rejecting you. Let's just watch her."

Sure enough, she went all the way around and stopped where she started. Then she walked over to Dianne, put her muzzle to her heart, and then put her nose to the ground as if she was eating the dirt. And I knew she wasn't, but it looked like she was eating the dirt. Then she put her nose back to Dianne's heart and she looked at me. I said, "Boy, Tory, I'm not following you."

And she did it again, she repeated that; and the third time, Tory was frustrated with me. She took a big sigh, she reached down, and took an actual bite of the dirt. And I thought, *"What is she doing?"* I said, "Dianne, now do you know what she's showing you?" And she started to cry. She said, "When the babies were starving, they would sit on the ground naked, starving with their little bellies sticking out, near death, and just eat sand. And the sand made them feel full. And of course, it killed them, but the sand made them feel full, so even the mothers would give the babies dirt to eat to keep them quiet... and to settle their stomachs down." Of course, now we're all losing it, right?

Then, Tory took her foreleg—and I have 14 people who witnessed this, by the way, because it just sounds like the wildest story, but all the women that were there were like, "Wow." She took her foreleg—and when a horse paws the ground, there's a rhythm to it—but instead, she extended her foreleg way out, and then just drew it back, kind of in a straight line. She did that four or five times. And I said to Dianne, "What is she showing you now?" And she said, "Okay, now your horse is kind of freaking me out." And I said, "What?" She said, "They buried their babies in the sand by hand. Those mothers would get on all-fours themselves, and just draw this straight trench back until it was deep enough to hold the baby's body, put the baby in, and cover it with sand."

So, wow, right?

M.H. Yeah.

M.P She asked, in fact, "Why is your horse showing me this?" And I said, "I believe because she wants you to

110

know that you are heard. That you are really heard. That she saw the images you carried in your mind, she felt the sadness you still carry to this day in your heart, she saw it, she heard it, and it's cross-species sadness, right?" And she was very moved, she ended up, of course, crying on Tory's shoulder and feeling so affirmed that it was as big a story, and it was as traumatic as what she had always felt that it was. It opened the gateway to the rest of her work with me.

To me, these horses give me incredible information—and I call that pantomime. Many of my horses pantomime. You know, they'll give me these big pantomime things that they're doing to show me what they're seeing... so—that was the second story.

M.H. That was the second story, assuredly. Do you find certain horses are more drawn to the work? And the second question, are certain breeds?

M.P. I personally feel that a lot of the somatic energy body work is done by the Gypsy Vanners in a very different way from any other breed. And I am a fan of Gypsies—but that's kind of why—because I think they're almost one cell off the fairy realm in how they can understand the pure body somatics.

It's usually been my Quarter horses and Paints and Arabs that have been the big pantomimers. They've been the ones that are more attuned to the direct images people will send from their mind's eye to the horse. And so, I'm kind of a fan of those breeds for that.

But I do find—I've worked with Haflingers—I've worked with a lot of different breeds, and all of them are good. The only horses I find who don't want to do this work, are ones in which I say the covenant between man and horse has been broken. So, I totally believe in repurposing rescue horses where we can. You know those horses that we have brought back into good health, and they're in a good state. But so many of those rescue horses...they don't owe us anything. I mean, mankind has starved them, or beaten them, or worse. And for those, I honestly am against people adopting rescue horses for this kind of work, because unless they're clear that this horse's covenant with mankind is not broken, then I think it's fine, but if it is, they just deserve our tender loving care for the rest of their life. They shouldn't be asked to do something for us, right?

Most of the time, my own horses have had golden childhoods, you know. They've been well taken care of, and well-fed, and well-loved, and well-trained, and so they're happy to do the work and to help mankind. I think all breeds do it, and all horses can do it. Just for me, there's something about those Gypsies that are unbelievable in that Reiki Chakra—you know, that whole...the whole somatic picture. They're uncanny. They're really uncanny.

M.H. Yeah. My Reiki Master works with a cancer workshop that goes on once a month. It's free...

M.P. Nice.

M.H...but there are counselors there, and a Reiki Master. And the horse that she works with is a Gypsy Vanner, so...

M.P. Yup. There's something—they just do something—they just feel it differently. They're just really tuned in and turned on by the human vibration.

M.H. Well, she said that—she's a communicator, too—and she said the horse told her, "We are from the angelic realm, and this is our job."

M.P. Yeah. Yup, exactly. Exactly.

M.H. OK, at some point, you decided to train people in this technique. How did that come about?

M.P. In the end of 2008, I suddenly had a series of different people emailing, or calling the office, or coming in to see me who asked if they could apprentice with me. And it was all within 30-days. Like, nobody had asked that before, and then all of a sudden, boom, boom, boom, boom. And I really listen to the Universe, so I felt that

that was my spirit saying, "Hey, guess what? This is the next piece of your calling."

And it was. It needed to be in my heart, Mary—that I was to a point in my practice where I could unselfishly and 100 percent—with 100 percent transparency, right—train other people to do the work I was doing. That was important. I took another—I don't know—three or four weeks to kind of meditate on it and think on it because I didn't want to be a trainer that—and there are trainers out there that do this—that say, "Well, I'm going to show you all of this, but I'm not going to show you the really good stuff because I want to keep that for myself." I wanted to make sure I was not in that self-absorbed place, but instead willing to say, "Everything I know, everything I am, everything I have, you may have." And that's when I knew I was supposed to do it. We began it at the end of 2008. And it's been blessed ever since.

M.H. Who do you find is drawn to become a practitioner?

M.P. Primarily women: we do have male graduates, but primarily women. Primarily mid-life, it's kind of a—not always, but kind of—the majority of our students are second career, or in their 40s and 50s, so they've got some maturity on them. They find a deep calling to make a difference in the world. And the thought of being able to spend more time with their horse and make a difference in somebody's life is just exactly what they want to do.

Most of our students come into the program not even truly knowing what it is, so I do believe it's a spirit thing; it's a divine thing because so many of them—they're in this thing a good four or five months before they really get why they're here—it's like their calling catches up with them afterwards, right? They come in and they start learning so much, and so much about themselves and people and human dynamics, and all these things. And they get really excited, you know like, "Wow, this is—I wasn't sure what I got myself into," you know.

I do think Spirit hands us the best of people, and in a super fun way. They sort of show up and they're not sure why they're here. I just did an intake on a new student, who starts with us in January, this morning and she said, "Can I ask you a crazy question?" I said, "Sure." She said, "Do all the other students know why they're in this program?" And I started to laugh, and I said, "No, they have no clue, they just know they're supposed to be here." She goes: "Oh, I feel so much better because I just feel like I'm supposed to do this. I just know I am," ... but she said, "I've never worked with you, I've never seen your work, but I just know you're my teacher." I'm like, "Okay." So kind of fun.

M.H. Is it always horse people?

M.P. No. We have a second program we opened in January 2018, that is the Gestalt Coaching method for people who do not have horses and aren't interested in building it through the horses. They just want to be an excellent coach and they want to learn the Gestalt methodology.

But even in our EGC—even in our equine gestalt therapy—probably, I don't know, three or four percent of the people who come in did not own a horse before. They're attracted to horses, but they don't even know how to put a halter on. You know, they're just at that level. They learn all that in here, but that's not—they just knew somehow that horses were magical beings and they wanted to work with them. And they come in kind of shy about that part, but you know, they want to see what it is.

Yeah, so that's where I think they don't have to be horsemen, they can learn because it's on the ground, it's not riding, and you know they can learn the basics of all that, and usually they have a handler that can do that kind of thing anyway.

M.H. I only have two more questions.

M.P. Okay.

M.H. Three actually, but they're short.

M.P. Okay.

M.H. Maybe.

M.P. Your questions are short, my answers are long.

M.H. It's all good. I love it. Was there a particular horse that showed you the way?

M.P. Yes. There were actually two. One was a mare I had when I was in Flagstaff in the mid-80's, and her name was Riddle. Big sorrel Quarter Horse mare. And she had been one of our brood mares. We bred Paints for a million years. And she was one that was very much— very mare-y. You know she—the geldings are usually the people ponies, right? They are like all over people and the mares sometimes can be a little bit more introverted and kind of standoffish, and that was her personality. She really wasn't one that was, like, all over people. And yet, she was the one that in Flagstaff, I would see my clients, who were not horsemen, take a walk up our driveway, just to stretch their legs and kind of get their mind clear. And she'd come over to the fence and spend so much time with them. They weren't feeding her anything, they weren't even... and the way our fences were, they could-n't even really scratch more than just her face. And yet, she'd stand there with them for an amazing length of time.

117

And then when the client came back to me to do the second part of a session, or a second session of that day, their whole energy field was shifted, and their emotions were so affected by just this interaction with her that I thought, "Hmm, maybe muggles—maybe non-horse people—get the benefit of horse healing too." You know? I knew we as horsemen did, because I had plenty of girlfriends that had breast cancer and swore their horse was the one who got them through it, but the fact that people who really didn't know one end of a horse from another were so affected and so moved was an amazing thing.

So, Riddle, the big sorrel mare, was one, and the other was a horse I called Scooter, and Scooter really opened me up to tying in the—not only the Gestalt, but all the somatics work. He was a little Paint, a little Paint reining horse, nothing—no Gypsy, no exotic blood—and he was mind-blowing in the way he would pantomime to me. And I would think, "That horse is acting things out for me." He was really my first "pantomimer" years ago. And it was undeniable. People would watch him work and say, "Gosh, I mean he might as well be giving you sign language. He's just acting out whole little things for you to pick up on."

And he also did all my—he was my early, what I call "equi-detector," so he could tell if people were telling themselves the truth or not. And he would give me a very clear indication. And all my horses have ever since, but I'm not sure I would have seen it, you know? I mean, you wonder what you—you and I right now—we wonder what we don't know to even ask, right?

M.H. Right.

M.P. They're just opening so much. And opening our eyes so swiftly, and it's because those two horses showed me so many different things, I'm excited about what others will show me. It could be behaviors they've all been doing for a million years, right?

M.P. But now that we've translated it, and we've woken up to it, now we see it, you know? So that's my belief. I think probably some old cowboy on the range in 1800s made his bed roll up and laid down and his horse was leaching (pulling negative energy off), or pantomiming, or doing a thousand other balancing chakras, you know, and he'd be like, "I don't know what you're doing, get off me, stupid horse, go away." And the horse is like, "I can really help you out, dude. If you would just let me." So it's kind of fun, yeah.

By this time one question was top of mind. For me, there was no question the horses were doing all these things—I had seen it and felt it for myself. But the abiding question was why.

M.H. Why do you think horses choose to help us heal?

M.P. I think because they know we're in a lot of trouble. I think because they know we're getting further—as a culture—we're getting further and further away from understanding our emotions, understanding that we're here for joy, understanding that we're here for finding peace and finding joy. And as we, as a culture, just get further and further and further away from that and are more intellectual, and "headier", and more out of touch with really what we're here for, to experience, I think they're reaching out, maybe too late, but they're reaching out to kind of go, "Wow, human beings, come on, focus with me here and be here." I don't think they're the only animal doing that, I think there are other animals doing that, and I think they realize that the entire planet is being led and imploded by this species that is the least contactful with Mother Earth that there is.

And I think if I were a horse, and I was going, "Wow, you guys are in charge of everything, and you're really screwed up. This is not good for me, it's not good for my fellow horses because you guys are somehow in charge around here, and look what you're doing to the planet, and to yourselves, and to the very experience of joy and being in the moment." So, I think they're making a sort of, last ditch effort to reach us.

And you know, God bless Jane Goodall for showing us that the apes were more than just hairy beasts, right? And people that have worked with the dolphins, and you know, just many, many animals have stepped up to try and say, "Could you please realize why we're really here on this earth. And could you please move toward joy. "So that's my thought, anyway. As crazy as that sounds, that's what I think they're doing.

M.H. Wow. I think that is the perfect way to finish this out. I so deeply appreciate it, and I won't be crying. Much.

M.P. Well, have a blessed day, my friend, you bet. And—go nuzzle a muzzle until your own muzzle is around you, so find muzzles to nuzzle.

[Chapter 25]

On The Buckle

It's a horseman's term. Reins, attached on either side of a bit, circle up into your hands. As you mount, you grab mane and the reins, hopefully with some measure of ease, and then try to quiet your hands down. To quiet everything down, some days.

The reins, among other aids, are your voice talking— through leather and metal, through tension and release to this most sensitive spot of your horse's physical being. The lips. The mouth. The jaws.

Here, you can speak to them. Stop. Go forward. Turn. Move up.

While every other part of your body is scrubbing away, heels or legs asking for a gait change or a bend, torso leaning forward and asking for the same, or hips sitting deep and grounded saying easy. Easy.

But nothing quite says relax, my friend, we're good, our workday is done like being on the buckle. Those reins, circling up from the bit, are joined at the top by a fastener. Leather slides over and through a buckle. And Bob's your uncle. Everything is connected. But not really. Not until you mean it.

I often, but not often enough, wonder what would happen if I talked to myself as I meant to talk to my horse.

What if, knowing the great rewards of kindness, I dropped the reins? Or just enough...

I'm trying, as if I were a horse, once again to understand.

What glimmers in the distance?

What might yet be possible?

What if I lived my life...on the buckle?

At least long enough to take a deep breath, start again and never forget.

[Chapter 26]

End Days. Also Known As A Beginning

My Reiki Master told me, after I told her I was heading home to NC, that this was often the case. That as folks approached, attained their Master Attunement and began that journey—they would undertake a physical journey as well. To somewhere, maybe to the other side of the world. I wasn't going quite so far. North Carolina. Friends from the School of the Arts were gathering there. Relatives already lived there. And that green, green grass was calling. Everything fell into place so easily. A buyer showed up before my house was even on the market. A house, the perfect house in NC showed up in my email. Even though I had no mortgage letter in place, we scorched through the process and in 24 hours, on my mother's birthday, despite the four other bids, the house was mine.

There was an elaborate plan to get See and his not great ankles to NC. He would not be on a trailer more than 6 hours a day. He would then have a day or two off, depending on how he was doing. This sounds like there would be a trailer available whenever he was ready—but that is so not the case. Arranging this sort of thing for horses is not the same as booking travel for people.

Once a horse was dropped off at a transport barn, who knew when the next trailer would come along. It would probably set a record for the slowest—and one of the most expensive—transfers ever. But I would do anything to have my friend with me, as long as he was safe...

The move was less than 10 days away. There was no turning back. For me. There was a call from Randy, Micca's mother.

Randy managed to punch the message in quickly. "Seymour is lame. He can't make the trip. Ever." She hung up while I had just started to howl.

The next day I met the vet and Micca at the barn. I had more or less accepted that he couldn't travel but as I listened to the evaluation and discussion, I realized something else was going on. This was a quality-of-life discussion. This was a "is it time to let See go?" discussion. I turned to Micca.

"Mary, he was bad yesterday. I couldn't stand to make him go on in that kind of pain. I asked them to come look. "

The vet tech was trotting around with him. Seymour was moving ok at this point I thought. Not limping. Not exactly stepping out but no different to the other times he'd gone lame. I turned back to the vet. He had figured out I'd been blind-sided. In all fairness, I think the phone call with Randy was supposed to make this clear before I went off my head. But the vet's assessment was good—or as good as it would get. See would stay at Winsome. We would re-assess as necessary...

I said "goodbye" to See before the day Jasper and I left for NC. There was so much going on that I wouldn't have time to do it properly on any other day. So, there we were again, saying goodbye only this time outdoors with a backdrop of Pike's Peak. At Winsome Farms, you could take the long view easily, looking out over the valley to the Rampart Range and the rest of the 14'ers beyond. It is a restful view—and we had done this before. This whole goodbye thing. Hell, See chose this, his own moment. Now moving fairly well, he chose to stay at a time when I could no longer change course. My Colorado house was locked into a sale for a few days hence. And the North Carolina home would close a week later. Just enough time to drive, rest up and recover from this.

Most of all "this" was physically separating from Seymour.

That day, mainly we were just together. I would lean on him and hug him. He would lay his head on my shoulder. We breathed together. I would press my face into his bear of a neck, still thick with his winter coat and draw comfort from his scent as I always had. Then we would hug some more. Inevitably, there had to be a time to step away. To walk on but keep looking back until he was no longer in view.

My beloved. My oh so beloved See.

The thing was, I could still feel him. Hell, some of the time I could still smell him. I could tell he was still working beside me. I quickly came to believe this was the training time when I could still reach him, touch into him before he went farther away. A way to learn how to reach him even then.

It was a year plus a little like this. To learn not to panic, but to stay steady and breathe. And trust. He was still there. Still there.

Micca and I had a code. Pretty sure we all did. I would answer the phone and she would quickly say:

It's not that call.

Until of course it was.

~

My son had been back home for some weeks, working on the final details of his dissertation and preparing for its defense. He already had a job offer, only dependent on that successful defense. But his journey east had not been easy either. Our beloved Aunt Jo had passed away, and Jasper was desperately trying to get here in time for her funeral. But his animal companion Wiley, an older, rescued shepherd—and official best dog ever—was not faring well on a cross country journey either.

~

My sister and brother-in-law were here for the funeral after their own crazy trip from Colorado, but the real crazy didn't start until they were on the ground. High winds and driving rain had made it nearly impossible to even know which road we were on.

No matter which way I looked, storm clouds were building.

~

In Arizona, where Jasper and Wiley had found each other, where they started their journey together years before, they held up for a day to give Wiley a rest, a chance, but this extraordinary dog's time was coming to a close. As Jasper's college friend desperately drove for the emergency vet, Wiley, wrapped in the true comfort of Jasper's arms, slipped away.

~

Some weeks later, we're at the phone call with Micca.

Jesse, horse care person extraordinaire at Winsome, found Seymour laboring in the morning and reached out to Micca.

And she called me. His temperature was up. His respiration was up. His heart rate was twice what it should be. Yes, we should call the vet. She was off the phone at once, and the waiting began.

Apart from those dodgy ankles, Seymour had never been a high-maintenance horse. I had every reason to believe he would be with me for a long time—one way or the other. I had almost every reason to believe he would beat this too. But that wasn't what my heart was telling me. It said hold steady. Stay the course. Much like what I was saying to myself in that first goodbye. Only not.

I knew this time I had to stay steady for all of us—and he did too. Deep beneath the waves of fear and even panic, deep beneath his struggles and deep beyond all the miles, I could feel him. I took a deep breath and then another.

The phone rang.

The vet was there. A woman this time that I didn't know from when I lived in Colorado. She was kind. "Yes, we could wait to see if he could ride this out. Even another day in case it made a difference. Not a problem. We could try to make him comfortable."

I asked to speak to Micca again. I wasn't really asking for advice—just a grounding in this situation. I needed to know how it compared with times before. I needed to know—better, worse, different? But really, I just needed a little more time to be certain. To know that what I was hearing, feeling, seeing was not just a hustling panic. To know it was time, and that once again he was making that decision. My beloved. The Mighty. See.

~

It was time.

Of course, it doesn't happen with this kind of drama or dispatch. Arrangements had to be made. And other hearts had to be protected. His herd. His friends. His peppermint mafia.

The vet gave him a shot to relax and began to move him to the back of the property. The phone rang again, and this time I was totally unprepared. Stella, Flo's mother, See's champion for so long, was driving to the barn. " I am coming; I am coming to Seymours."

Like another dear friend, she often referred to him in the plural.

I had no idea how to answer, how to put this. Here was poor Stella, heading to the barn to get him out for a bath or a graze or both—

"Stella, we have to let him go—they're going to put him down..."

But she knew. She had asked Micca to call if there came a time to let him go.

And now she was driving hell for leather so he would not be alone, without a close friend.

~

There was almost a wind inside my house. A breeze. A draft. It was sudden, like air kicked up against the foothills. At the core of it was an unmistakable scent, as if once again, one last time, he had just wrapped his neck around me...

It was 2:16 PM on June 28th, 2018. And Seymour was gone.

[Chapter 27]

A New Hello

We all lose that which we love. Those whom we love. We are all unique in our pain and loss. We are all achingly the same. How can this be? When each story proclaims this: a unique life has roared across the stage, fully charged, imperfectly realized, but wholly alive. And then gone... How?

I had thought he would live forever, or at least on and on to a ripe old age. To be fair, I thought the same of myself and everyone else I loved. Slowly but surely (or in some cases smacked upside the head hard and fast) it occurred to me that I was wrong. That hope and answers had fused to an unfortunate degree.

When I thought about moving to NC, I saw a clinic where See and I would practice, together. When that dream fell apart, I found I could reach out to him, to his still very close presence and that his energy would be there for me. But was that still the case?

Now, I wanted to stand fast in the near ruins of what I believed. Energy goes on. Folks, beings go on, though they have transitioned. Therefore, See was still there in some form of existence.

But here was the catch—integral to those beliefs was the certainty that Seymour was a sovereign being. That our work together was a choice made by each of us, serving together. So what now? Had his spirit dispersed into the grandeur of the universe? Or was this a time of rest before he returned in some form or another? Or was it possible that this great spirit would still find a way to be, to work with me—but did I even have the right to ask him?

It was the last question that troubled me the most.

I was enormously grateful to him for everything he had been to me. The inspiration of his talent and beauty. The grounding of his humor and presence, even from afar. The moment I turned around and saw him for what and who he truly was. The ongoing amazement that this fabulous creature, this wondrous being actually loved me.

Had he not given me enough? In what universe could I ask for more? Finally, I turned to the best animal communicator I knew—or more fairly knew of.

Anna Twinney.

Founder of Reach Out to Horses, Anna is also known for her work with Mustangs—and Premarin foals. For her work as a Reiki Master. She is an International Equine Specialist, Natural Horsemanship Clinician and kind friend of any other horse that needs to be heard.

With all our connections, I trusted her.

I had met her briefly at that "From Fear to Love" seminar with Melisa Pearce up around Boulder. We had crossed paths at Zuma's Rescue Ranch in Littleton more than once. Her reputation was stellar, and I had vowed if I ever really needed an animal communicator—and now I did—I would call on her.

The process was not complicated. She needed two pictures, without humans. No problem. See, a photographers' favorite, was well represented. Even trying to find the best, the most essential shot of Seymour was a happy occupation.

That was a good thing. I had been told that there would be a wait, most likely a substantial one and the warning did not lead me astray. I started the process in July. We were finally scheduled to meet by telephone October 31st, 2018—although to be fair I had missed a last-minute opening in early September. But surely Halloween, the time when the veil between the living and those on the bridge is supposed to be the thinnest, was a perfect time to reach out.

Anna explained the process to me first.

I would listen silently while she connected with See for the initial download from him. She would also listen in silence. Then, she would relate what she "heard" and "saw"— and then I could ask questions.

The initial download was also to give Anna a grounding in who this creature was.

Anna Twinney:

"I think majestic is the word, or noble, that would describe him best. I'm gonna describe physical I have him as a larger individual. Larger, you know.

"And he shows himself as quite, *quite* a strong minded, male.

"A talented individual that I would class, either central to south, but not quite all the way south in Germany.

"I think he's showing me here dressage moves...with his majestic being, which I think he is. I can see "collection." I can see him figuring things out by himself. Imagine watching an individual move where you see him trotting in one spot. Or he's cantering in one spot at something about, um...how he holds and carries himself. But then the next thing I see is quite a talented jumper. I don't think it was kept to the arena alone. I do think he has many aspects in which he sees himself as an athlete.

"So, what he shows me is highly talented, great mind, great athlete...

"Awesomely put together confirmation wise

"Quite the posture he has. And a lineage that has the performance.

'I see him leaving Germany in a proud manner, knowing that he has a career ahead.

I don't have this fellow looking back and regretting things. I don't have him looking back saying he was exported from Germany or moved from Germany without his will. I don't think that at all.

'He'd have been bred and groomed to have a career and was quite happy with it. For some reason, he's not looking back saying anything was out of his hands or people were controlling him or it was against his wishes. Everything smooth. That's how I have it...quite confident in the knowing that his life was gonna turn out okay."

While we weren't yet at answers to my questions, I found it deeply grounding to hear all this. He had been happy. He never looked back. And he was, even from the bridge, the same confident, occasionally majestic creature that I had known. But there was more. I had told Anna about losing both parents to Alzheimer's before See arrived...

AT:

Definitely a hard course of yours. And I think potentially at some point, you wondered how, how on earth he could fall into your lap like that. You know, were you worthy of who he is? Absolutely. You are. And absolutely a big piece, for the fact that I don't, I just don't think he looked back when he met you, Mary. I think he looked forward, which is huge.

MH:

I have this book that I was working on, about how horses heal and, I wanted the last chapter to be Seymour and the amazing things that he could do, how he healed people, that is. And I kind of stalled out. Once I moved here, to North Carolina it was hard for me to keep it going. So, I wondered if there was some wisdom there, from him?

AT:

I can tell you right away, as you're speaking, you're probably...you're likely stalling because you're coming from your head.

You know, if you allow yourself to channel, you won't stall that chapter.

His answer to you is *channel.*

Have you put in there the chapter about you healing your heart?

MH: No.

AT: Is there a reason you left that out?

MH:

Um, I haven't really completed the outline for it. I've been interviewing people because I wanted a wide view on all those different ways to heal. But, I mean, that was my original concept for it. So maybe it's time to....Yes, it is. It's time to open that description.

AT:

He was with you close to 10 years, 15 years,

But it looks like he's choosing to walk with you, which is cool.

So what? What else would you like me to ask him or say to him or share with him?

MH:

Well, I mean, if he is willing to keep walking with me, if I can reach out to him, call out to him, whenever.

I mean, I just didn't know if I had the right. If it was fair.

AT:

No, it's absolutely fair.

And he's also showing a crystal that you work with.

So, I'm going to share with him. I'm gonna say that you were cautious about what was, or what was not fair. And I'm going to tell him that he brought great clarity around that, and that you understand his messages and that knowing that you can bring him through and bring him into your heart will not only help you now but also all that is yet to come. And I'm also going to tell him I'm hoping he is hearing all of that. I'm saying that you're looking to continue with the book. It looks like it's a work in progress. And there's more to come and expansion needed. That might take you longer than you think but it's certainly worth expanding. Okay?

There was one more thing; strangely I haven't been able to find it in the transcript. But I know I heard it.

And now I realize, I heard it straight from him, and that was the reason it was so clear.

See, the Mighty, the sacred clown, the jump master, the healer, and my friend, said this:

I will walk with you—

I will walk you home.

Sometimes it is necessary
to re-teach a thing its loveliness.
Galwell Kinnell

[Chapter 28]

Horse Heroes

In the months and years since I started working on this book, so many things have happened. I did move to North Carolina and started caring for rescue horses. While I've yet to establish the sanctuary practice I had hoped for with Seymour, I have learned to trust my own communication with animals—at least a little.

I have learned to listen.

And I've learned of the amazing gift of hearing their story and telling it back to them.

~

Sometimes, standing by the fence and listening, one can hear the most extraordinary stories told.

Not the ones of loss and despair.

I remember hearing Jodi Messenich, of Zuma's Rescue Ranch in Colorado, say they never told the horses' backstories in front of them or even nearby. Since these were often accounts of physical and emotional abuse, or the horrors of unbelievable neglect, I couldn't help but agree with her and have tried to stay true to it. But as time went by, these other stories began to rise to the surface.

Tales of hope, happiness and of that one time when someone loved them.

I have found and offered comfort in re-telling discarded horses their true stories, the ones they've hidden inside but still hold and cherish.

They, like all of us, want to know they were worth it.

As with most things equine, I began to learn the truth of this with Seymour. While he was by no means discarded or abused, towards the end of his career he ended up in a new barn. Although they were loving and welcoming, no one there knew about his glory days the way they had in his previous barn. Always his advocate, I would tell his story to anyone who would listen. It was Randy Henry who pointed out that the one who really loved hearing his story—was him. When I looked more closely, I could see his body shift. His head got higher, even as the arch came back in his neck. His chest lifted; he gained a hand or so and voila, the "Seymour at a competition" persona was back. Gifted, graceful and proud. I had seen this transformation before, but now the dots connected.

Stories are healing. They are transformational.
But they are also best when grounded in more examples.

So let me begin to introduce you to a few of my new friends....

Bucky. A liver chestnut with a flaxen mane. Small, with one eye nearly blue. Sturdy. Stand-offish, but with an anxious aspect. A worn place on his face where a too small halter was left on too long.

Still. I can hear his story. See it too...

How children thrilled to see this one-time circus pony enter the ring with his tricks and his beauty—and how they loved to greet him after, this star who once had kindness in his eyes.

And his pasture mate, Bailey, a proud and mischievous Saddlebred. Now, with his bowed back and withered hindquarters, one has to really look to see this is a warrior of grace. Call it out so he can remember it too. That he is a creature of fire and whimsy and the pure joy of movement.

Still.

Bucky told me more of his story when I subbed in with the boys one day. Usually stand-offish, he stood in front of me and now clearly wanted my attention. I asked him if he wanted to tell me a story, and he began to blow air through his lips and nod. So, here's what he told me. He had another role at the circus, one which he had assigned himself. Much like in electricity, he was the ground for the other animals. He helped them to be calm, and steady, even in their most difficult circumstances. He held their space. He held their hope. It was a great gift he offered—and I imagine it wasn't always easy, because he himself had to be the most steadfast of all.

He was wonderfully proud of it; one could feel his whole soul there as he told this most loving story.

But there was more to come.

A few days later, I was out at another barn to learn groundwork for holistic horsemanship. I knew the train-

142

er Charity from my early days volunteering for H.E.R.O., a Winston Salem rescue. Merida and I were also "old" friends; she was one of the horses I Reiki'd when I first came to NC.

We were on a little break—one of many, I fear I must admit—when I started telling Charity this story. Immediately, Merida started nodding her head up and down and blowing as well. Out of the corner of my eye, I caught exactly the same movement—from Rayne Bow, the brand-new rescue I hadn't even met yet. I looked at Charity, like oh my god they know! I said, I think they like his story—and dang if they didn't nod their heads and blow again—both of them! So, you never really know who you're telling the stories to, or why—or who needs to hear them.

But here's the thing. Stories need to be told. And heard. Acknowledged.

Burnished, even, so a soul can shine.

In the end it doesn't really matter if it's a rescue, or an aging friend.

A young one looking for a safe way forward.

A wild one looking for a way back.

A racer looking for glory lost, or a success never found.

Or just your horse, heart horse or lesson horse or no.

I do this because rescues, and every four-leg, needs to connect to a version of themselves which is not to be pitied. Which is valiant and true and kind.

They all have stories, and, in those stories, they are stars. Seeing themselves in a new light, they shine.

Listen and tell them, out loud to them and then to others. Tell them simply or with every yearning, joyful exhortation.

Tell them with the sweet scent of grass and oats and the molasses laden smell of Senior intermingled.

Tell them on just a regular old day, standing by the fence.

Tell them all their stories.

They need to know themselves, once again, as heroes.

[Chapter 29]

Epilogue

For all the anecdotes, for all the science, for all the preponderance of history detailing a relationship almost beyond measure, in the end horses are a measure of the heart. Of the senses. Of the sense of being here in this world, grounded and secure, wild and adventurous, hurting and barely holding on—but whole.

They speak to you of yourself, of your hopes and fears. Of your memories. Of that which is beyond memory. They speak to you of who you've always been.

You are 6. If you're lucky, your grandfather has a pony—a one-time circus pony. Champ is kind, and clever, and surprisingly fast. He will teach you. And the kindness of a horse's heart will not be the least of it.

You're 10. You've eaten eggs every single morning for two weeks. Now, for one full hour, 60-ish golden minutes you'll be out at Oxon Hill Stables for a glorious trail ride. The next morning, it starts all over again. And lasts until you finally have your own horse, years later.

You will finally learn to like eggs again, many more years later.

You're 13. You've saved as long as you can remember. No mean feat when you count it out in quarters. Now, you're sitting on the ground while your horse, the absolute object of your desire, trots merrily off to the far end of the ring. It's the second time you've been on her back. And the first time you've been dumped on the ground. But no matter. Before these years are done, you'll be a cowgirl, and trick-rider, a Paleo jockey and an Indian and a phantom in the mist of an early summer morning.

You are 60. If you're lucky, your heart horse stands beside you, his muzzle tucked in your hand. But in his clever eyes, mischief is afoot. He may not have known you when you were 6, or 10 or 13, but he knows you now. And this "now" tucks every one of those years inside it.

You're 72. Your brilliant boy stands beside you in spirit—and as steady and present as ever. In this "now" is every moment of ever.

In gratitude, you are blessed.

In gratitude...

ACKNOWLEDGEMENTS

As in any undertaking—especially one that's taken this long—there are a number of people to thank...

To Elizabeth Lord and Alec Nesbitt for their wonderful pictures.

To Stacey Briggs for creating the cover I dreamed about.

To Robert Neuwoehner for his patience dealing with a newbie while formatting my manuscript as an ebook.

I am very grateful to the Immortals Flo Schomorgoner and Samantha Cook for their support when I was just beginning to ride again, and for all the fun at the shows. To Flo especially for her ongoing support of The Mighty. To Stella Gimpilova, Flo's mom, especially for her loving attention to See in that final year, and on that final day. I am deeply grateful.

For all the friends from all the barns, I am very grateful for your support and patience. Also, for all the fun times!

For those who loved Seymour too, especially Addi and family. Anyone who not only takes great care of the boy but also decorates your trunk for Christmas deserves a special shout-out. For Deb Ettenger O'Connor for persisting with Seymour's spa day even when he tried to deafen her.

For Mary and Alison Paschall for so much.

For Melissa Ball's kind attention to See when I could not be there.

For Jesse—Horse Magician and a great friend of See. And for the whole Henry family, Micca, Bill and Randy— much love and gratitude.

And of course, to Sam and Rachel Konigsberg— without your generosity there would be no See in my life.

For new friends met online in various classes. Thank you, Anna Bergenstrahle, Ulrike Berzau and all. Your constant requests for "more" to read meant everything to me—not to mention spurring me on, if you will. And now—here you go!

To Ann Baldwin and Anna Twinney—thank you for taking my calls. To Melisa Pearce, your inspiration has woven in and out of all my horse time in Colorado and beyond.

To Devon...oh my! I thank you for your story, your wise counsel, your encouragement, your beautiful horses—and for telling me about Heartland!

To Erin Keefe-Feinner, thank you for re-igniting my Reiki journey on so many levels.

To Kathleen and all my beloved NCSA alumni. Just so happy to be around you now for so many reasons but needing no reason at all.

To my family here in NC on both sides. What a font of unconditional love—no matter!

And someday we'll even gather together again.

To Grady and Ben. How I would love to sit around that table many more times, laughing. And to Alec, for lingering there to hear one more story about The Mighty.

And to Ulrike, again, for helping me navigate the wilds of Kindle Direct. (And by golly, yes, I do want a best-seller!)

To my son Jasper, who has always supported my writing and me. Also, for insisting on helping to drive across the country, more than once. And for making me laugh my arse off. Love you more than breath...

And to my sister Brenda. My encourager-in-chief from the beginning. Also, my Wise Eyes. And horse show companion. And business partner. And mischief partner, also from the beginning. And always, Seymour's great good friend.

But here in this arena, my sounding board, copy editor, layout designer, person who kept her eyes on the goal—and celebrator-in-chief when I would get it right. Violet and Grady would be so proud, even if one of their daughters still thought about setting up one more jump.

Maybe in the side yard...

ABOUT THE AUTHOR

After a career in television promotion, Mary returned to her first love—writing—and especially about horses. She now lives in Winston Salem, NC with her dog Lizzie Blue, cat Stormy Viola G, and lives in hope that she'll be joined by a heart horse here on this earth again someday, knowing The Mighty will always walk with her.

Appendix: Notes

---

1. *Source:* Wikipedia
2. The Grand National is a National Hunt horse race held annually at Aintree Racecourse in Liverpool, England. First run in 1839, it is a handicap steeplechase over an official distance of about 4 miles and 2½ furlongs, with horses jumping 30 fences over two laps. *Source:* Wikipedia
3. Mindmonia
4. Yourdictionary.com
5. Linda Kohanov
6. All American Quarter Congress
7. The Eagala Model incorporates a licensed Mental Health Professional and a qualified Equine Specialist working together with horses and clients as equal partners in an experiential process that empowers life-changing outcomes.
8. Dr. Baldwin obtained her Bachelor's degree in Physics from University of Bristol, UK, her Master's degree in Radiation Physics from University of London, UK and her PhD in Physiology from Imperial College, University of London. She completed a two-year postdoc at College of Physicians & Surgeons, Columbia University, NY and then entered the faculty at the University of Arizona.

Made in the USA
Las Vegas, NV
13 November 2021

34381732R00097